The History of
MICHIGAN
WINES

The History of MICHIGAN WINES

150 Years of Winemaking along the Great Lakes

LORRI HATHAWAY & SHARON KEGERREIS

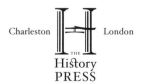

Charleston · London

THE History PRESS

Published by The History Press
Charleston, SC 29403
www.historypress.net

First published 2010
Second printing 2011

Manufactured in the United States

ISBN 978.1.59629.947.4

Library of Congress Cataloging-in-Publication Data

Hathaway, Lorri, 1969-
The history of Michigan wines : 150 years of winemaking along the Great Lakes / Lorri
Hathaway and Sharon Kegerreis.
p. cm.
Includes bibliographical references.
ISBN 978-1-59629-947-4
1. Wine and wine making--Michigan--History. 2. Wine and wine making--Great Lakes
Region (North America)--History. 3. Vineyards--Michigan--History. 4. Vintners--
Michigan--Biography. 5. Wineries--Michigan--Directories. I. Kegerreis, Sharon, 1968- II.
Title.
TP557.H38 2010
641.2'209774--dc22
2010019120

Dedicated to Michigan's hardworking winemakers; creative and passionate, and stewards of our land

CONTENTS

FOREWORD

The history of Michigan wines is just as fascinating as the wine industry of today. As the third-generation vintner of the state's oldest winery, St. Julian Wine Company, I'm proud to be part of an industry where the perseverance and passion of my grandfather and other winemakers paved the way to a vibrant future.

After the repeal of Prohibition, my grandfather relocated his winery from Ontario, Canada, to Michigan. At one time, I wished that he had kept traveling all the way to the Pacific Ocean rather than stopping along the shores of Lake Michigan. Not anymore! Michigan's unique climate created by a lake effect from the Great Lakes provides growing conditions that allow vineyards to flourish in our soils.

Our ancestors are indeed true pioneers of several facets of winemaking. Can you imagine planting, growing and harvesting grapes without the use of mechanical equipment, except for, perhaps, cutting shears? Can you fathom the kind of pumps, hoses, tanks, bottling equipment and even lack of refrigeration that challenged winemaking one hundred years ago? It was certainly a vigorous labor of growing the grapes and handcrafting the wine, though perhaps the most amazing feat, in retrospect, was distributing and selling the wine. Yet they accomplished it all—and accomplished it quite well, according to production statistics over the years.

One thing rings as true today for Michigan wineries as it did in the past: if you do not have strong, loyal market demand, you will not survive in the wine business. Michigan's early winemakers had to be market savvy, satisfying their customers just as we do today. As tastes of consumers changed, so did the varieties of grapes being grown and wines being produced. The state's wine industry continued to evolve through the decades to reach the fascinating place we are at today.

Michigan's current fraternity of vintners, now numbering in the seventies, is quite a determined, yet flexible and adaptable group of modern-day pioneers. Our region, though ideal for growing wine grapes, also presents us with some of the biggest wine-growing challenges of any region. We rise to meet these challenges every day, ultimately producing quality wines like no others. A tradition that began well over one hundred years ago is now a dynamic industry, producing award-winning wines that successfully compete with wines from all over the world.

The History of Michigan Wines is the first book documenting the state's spirited, yet turbulent, wine history. Lorri and Sharon take the reader on an intriguing journey through the development of Michigan wines with never-before-told stories and never-seen historical photographs of the industry's past.

The authors' in-depth research uncovers the state's first viable wine industry during the 1800s and a nationally leading industry in the first few decades following the repeal of Prohibition. This is shocking news to many who believe that the state's first wineries were established much later.

One thing stands true throughout the years: our vintners persevere time and again while facing hardships and challenges. The riveting stories of our state's wine history will give you a new appreciation for Michigan wines and the hard work and determination that goes into producing them.

David Braganini
St. Julian Wine Company

ACKNOWLEDGEMENTS

A special thanks to:

Dan Berger, wine writer
Dr. Kris Berglund, Michigan State University
Joe Borello, co-founder of Tasters Guild International
David Braganini, St. Julian Wine Company, grandson of Mariano Meconi
Karel Bush, promotion specialist, Michigan Grape and Wine Industry Council
Charles Catherman, St. Julian Wine Company (retired)
Elsa Corsi, daughter of John Corsi
Elsie Corsi, wife of Carl Corsi
Jim Corsi, son of John Corsi
John Corsi Jr., son of John Corsi
Rita Corsi, wife of Carl Corsi
Ellen and Tim Cote, Tabor Hill Winery (retired)
Sally Gagnon, daughter-in-law of twin Edward Gagnon
Andrea Grimes, cousin of David Braganini and coauthor of 2009
    release, Impronte
Dr. G. Stanley Howell, Michigan State University (retired)
Iron County Historical Museum
Linda Jones, program manager, Michigan Grape and Wine Industry Council
Amalia and Jason Julien and family
Philip Korson II, Cherry Marketing Institute

ACKNOWLEDGEMENTS

Bill Leonoff, Iron County Chamber of Commerce
Rick Moersch, founder of Round Barn Winery and former Tabor Hill winemaker
Monroe County Historical Museum
John Murch, son of Andy Murch
Dr. James O'Neill, collector of Temperance books
Stuart Pigott, European wine writer
Dr. Paolo Sabbatini, Michigan State University
Dick Scheer, owner of the Village Corner, Ann Arbor
Dr. Dennis Spinazze, son of Angelo Spinazze
Ernestine Spinazze, wife of Angelo Spinazze
Dr. Jerry Spinazze, son of Angelo Spinazze
Mario Spinazze, nephew of Angelo Spinazze, son-in-law of John Corsi
Kathleen Turan and family
Patti Vander Beek and family
Richard Vine, 1970s winemaker for Warner Vineyards
Rosemary Wade, daughter of Robert Wade
James J. Warner, Warner Vineyards, son of James K. Warner
Tim Washburn, Lawton Lions Community Center
Doug Welsch, Fenn Valley Vineyards
David Wozniak, grandson of Dr. Theodore Wozniak
Robert Wozniak, son of Dr. Theodore Wozniak
Robert Wozniak Jr., grandson of Dr. Theodore Wozniak

Especially, we thank our families for encouragement and support:

John Hathaway and children Anthony, Capri, Calli and Jack
Kris Kegerreis and children Julia and Makayla

GREAT LAKES, LATITUDE AND ATTITUDE

Michigan's wine history is a rollicking story, intricately interwoven and amazingly driven by a trio of key factors. First, massive lakes provide a tempering climate that enables a breadth of wine grapes and other agriculture to flourish in our soils. Second, the latitudes that run through hillside vineyards are shared with other renowned wine-growing regions of the world. Third, and most notably, our vintners are spirited, creative craftspeople and entrepreneurs—with, as one industry professional states, "a little bit of NASCAR in them." This combination of Great Lakes, geographic location and skilled winemakers has resulted in a vibrant 150-year winemaking legacy. *The History of Michigan Wines* features the never-before-documented wine history of our Great Lake State.

THE LAKES

Glacial movement thousands of years ago carved the basins of the Great Lakes and the landforms around them. Two mitten-shaped peninsulas, one very distinctly a mitten, are bordered by four of the five Great Lakes. Michigan's shoreline stretches 3,288 miles, making it one of the longest shorelines in the United States, second only to Alaska's. The Great Lakes are the largest surface of fresh water anywhere on earth, encompassing more than 94,000 square miles, or enough water to cover the continental United States under roughly ten feet of water.

As a result of several international treaties and statehood acts of the United States Congress, Michigan's borders reach to roughly the center of the lakes, encompassing 40.5 percent of the surface area of four of the five lakes: Michigan, Huron, Superior and Erie. Forty of the state's eighty-three counties touch at least one Great Lake, and regardless of where you stand in Michigan, you're always within eighty-five miles of a Great Lake. Further, there are eleven thousand inland lakes larger than 2 acres, one thousand of which are larger than 40 acres. In total, Michigan has 360,008 acres of lakes located within the two peninsulas. The lakes are a vibrant part of the Michigan lifestyle and have been since the first settlers arrived.

Early explorers first used Michigan's waterways as a means to travel into the New World. Settlers used the waterways for trading commodities, starting with the fur trade. It's no wonder that Michigan's early settlements— including Sault Ste. Marie, the Straits of Mackinac and Detroit—were along the Great Lakes. In 1681, Michigan first appeared on a French map as Lac de Michigani du Illinois, today's Lake Michigan. The word "Michigan" derives from the Algonquin language. "Michi" means great or large, and "gana" means lake or waters.

Fruits and, in particular, grapevines thrive here due to unique growing conditions created by prevailing westerly winds from Lake Michigan. The massive freshwater lake moderates seasonal temperatures, cooling the air in the summer and warming the air in the fall. This buffer on the climate extends the warmer growing season for regions located near the state's west coast, creating what is often referred to as a fruit belt. Grapes and a bounty of other fruits, like cherries, blueberries and apples, flourish—an agricultural windfall discovered by early explorers.

In the *1878 Annual Report of the State Horticultural Society of Michigan*, fruit grower Edward Bradfield of Ada touted, "We are satisfied that we are within the fruit belt. If you do not believe it, eat all the grapes you want, and taste some of my Iona grape wine."

Edward was responding to the query of what constitutes the fruit belt of Michigan. In the report, there are references suggesting that some believed "the fruit belt of Michigan is not an unknown or undiscovered country. There is a river in the ocean and there is a fruit belt by the lake shore. There are those who claim that the whole state is the belt itself—that there is but one belt, which is the state." From a purely nontechnical standpoint, we agree. Michigan is the second most agriculturally diverse state in the union, after all.

THE LATITUDE

The imaginary line that circles the world and lies halfway between the North Pole and the Equator connects world-class wine regions across the globe. The forty-fifth parallel is a prime location for growing and producing wine. This latitude weaves through the Bordeaux and Côtes du Rhône regions of France, Italy's Piedmont region and, yes, Michigan. Michigan's vineyards flourish between the forty-first and forty-seventh parallels. Compared to other wine regions along the forty-fifth parallel, Michigan's wine history is quite young.

THE ATTITUDE

Since the arrival of commercial winemaking in Michigan, winemakers have faced myriad challenges. The first commercial winemakers of the 1800s arrived by steamer to the Michigan Territory with, quite likely, just a few possessions. They settled in Monroe County and became business leaders in their communities in the New World. They grew successful, thriving wine operations that leveraged Michigan as a leading producer of wine in the nation, until the temperance movement and grape rot in the vineyards hindered wine production.

Within one month of the start of Prohibition, a national headline blasted, "U.S. Defied in Michigan," referring to multiple raids on Chianti-style wine in the Upper Peninsula. The Iron County state attorney refused to cooperate with federal officers, proclaiming, "These foreigners always have their grape presses and their homemade wine. They drink this in preference to water. They carry it to their work in their dinner pails and they won't work without it."

In the early 1900s, several European emigrants relocated to North America and continued Old World winemaking traditions in Ontario, Canada. Upon Prohibition's repeal in 1933, they immediately launched significant operations in Michigan. A dynamic new market opened with the legalization of commercial wine production, and entrepreneurial spirit led vintners to construct winemaking facilities with the capacities to produce as much as 1,000,000 gallons a year.

Through World War II, winemakers evolved their wines, using Michigan's agricultural bounty, and by the 1960s, they had collectively achieved production of 1,000,000 cases of wine per year. Unfortunately, in the 1960s and 1970s, lingering Prohibition-era regulations, a changing marketplace favoring table wines and an amended law that increased the costs of grapes wreaked havoc on the industry and shut down all except two of the state's wineries that had started in Michigan in the 1930s. The two that survived and remain open today are St. Julian Wine Company and Warner Vineyards (formerly Michigan Wineries).

In the meantime, innovative winemakers, like Angelo Spinazze of Bronte Champagne and Wine Company, and new pioneers, like Carl Banholzer and Leonard Olson of Tabor Hill Winery, Bernie Rink of Boskydel Vineyard and Edward O'Keefe of Chateau Grand Traverse, planted grape varietals that had not been grown in Michigan before. Michigan State University took on wine grape research in 1970, led by Dr. G. Stanley Howell for the next four decades. Significant plantings of French-American hybrids and European varietals provided the foundation for Michigan winemakers to reinvent the industry once again. And though wine production in the state was at an all-time low in the 1980s, table wine production was on the rise.

In the 1990s, Michigan winemakers began expanding the testing and planting of varietals in the state's soils. One winemaker, Dr. Charlie Edson of Bel Lago Vineyards on Leelanau Peninsula, has one hundred test varietals in his vineyard. Wally and Katie Maurer of Domaine Berrien Cellars in Berrien Springs tested many grapes for several years before selecting twenty-one varietals to produce their wine styles today.

Around the same time, wineries diversified to use the large amount of other fruits growing in the state. A new product introduction was fruit brandy, which was launched in the late 1990s thanks to a new law that enabled wineries to obtain small distiller licenses for a nominal fee. Since then, the industry has expanded its products, producing stylish eaux de vie (fruit brandies), vodkas, hard ciders and more using our agricultural bounty. More vineyards with vinifera and French-American hybrid grapevines were planted, and by 2000, wine production was on the rise again.

In the next decade, between 2000 and 2010, the number of wineries increased 300 percent to seventy-three wineries today. While Michigan's economy was a roller coaster, entrepreneurial vintners were ramping up winemaking operations throughout the state, in most regions of the Lower Peninsula and even into the Upper Peninsula.

Through the years, the state's winemakers were challenged by anti-business, Prohibition-era laws, high taxes and Mother Nature's fickle weather. Mother Nature has been known to throw hail, blow early frosts and delay spring, damaging grape harvests and orchard trees. For example, in 2009, a colder growing season made red wine production intricately difficult for our northern Michigan winemakers, though some of our southern Michigan winemakers believed the 2009 red vintage produced very fruit-forward, expressive wines. Just a few years prior, in 2005 and 2007, two of Michigan's stellar red vintages were produced. Consistently, year after year, our winemakers laugh in the face of Mother Nature and produce the finest world-class white wines.

Michigan's vintners ardently believe in the styles of wines they produce. Edward O'Keefe, founder of Chateau Grand Traverse in the northwest region of Old Mission Peninsula, was Michigan's earliest vocal proponent for producing world-class wines using European vinifera grapes. In the 1970s, he planted the state's largest commercial vineyard of European varietals to prove it. Our oldest winery, owned by David Braganini, grandson of St. Julian Wine Company founder Mariano Meconi, avidly believes that Michigan has a sweeter palate. The number one selling wine in Michigan, made with all Michigan grapes, is Blue Heron, a fruit-forward wine blend of Vidal, Seyval and Riesling produced by St. Julian.

"Wines can be dry without being overly acidic. They can be fruity without being sweet. If you don't want to taste fruit, drink scotch. It's all about producing a wine that is balanced," says Mike De Schaaf, a sixteen-year wine industry veteran who launched Hickory Creek Winery in 2005 with two business partners. His focus is on encouraging customers to think of wine as food. "Wine should be part of the dinner table."

FROM THE BEGINNING: WILD NATIVE GRAPEVINES

Vitis labrusca is a species of grapes native to the eastern United States. Wild and craggy native grapevines cascaded along riverbanks and intertwined with trees in this wild New World.

The first documented enjoyment of wine made with Michigan grapes occurred when René-Robert Cavelier, sieur de la Salle (La Salle), departed the Niagara region on August 7, 1679, commanding *Le Griffon*, a large sailing vessel, for the Upper Great Lakes. *Le Griffon* was the first large vessel to travel on Lake Erie and into Lake Huron and Lake Michigan and the second of La Salle's vessels to disappear. Remarkably, after 322 years, *Le Griffon* may have been found by the Great Lakes Exploration Group in 2001.

Four days after setting sail, the voyagers entered the straights (now known as the Detroit River) and sailed between the islands. Father Louis Hennepin, historian of the sailing party, recorded the region's beauty in his journal:

The islands are the finest in the world. They are covered with forests of nut and fruit trees, and with wild vines loaded with grapes. From these we made a large quantity of wine. The banks of the strait are vast meadows, and the prospect is terminated with some hills covered with vineyards, trees bearing good fruit; and groves and forests so well arranged that one would think that Nature alone could not have laid out the grounds so effectively without the help of man, so charming was the prospect.

Within two decades, Antoine de la Mothe, sieur de Cadillac, while serving as commandant at Michilimackinac, heard of the legendary region of the Rivière du Détroit (River of the Strait). Cadillac wrote to Count Frontenac, the governor of New France:

I have heard from the Indians and the coureurs de bois glowing descriptions of this fair locality…on both sides of this straight lie fine, open plains where the deer roam in graceful herds, where bears, by no means fierce and exceedingly good to eat, are to be found, as are also the savory [wild duck] and other varieties of game. The islands are covered with trees; chestnuts, walnuts, apples and plums abound; and, in season, the wild vines are heavy with grapes, of which the forest rangers say they made a wine that, considering its newness, was not at all bad.

Cadillac set sail for France in 1698 to convince Jérôme Phélypeaux, compte de Pontchartrain, minister of marine to Louis XIV (or his father, Louis), of the merits of a major settlement on the strait. When Cadillac arrived in the region, a ceremony to claim the land took place. In honor of the compte de Pontchartrain, Cadillac named the settlement Fort Pontchartrain du Détroit in 1701. (The post's name was shortened to Fort Détroit in 1751.) In a September 1702 letter to Count Pontchartrain, Cadillac wrote of the fort's progress, including the planting of a vineyard.

Around the late 1700s, early French voyagers paddled southwest from the Detroit River across Lake Erie, along what is now Michigan, and discovered vine-laden trees along the banks of a winding river through the land. They called the river *La Riviere au Raisin*, "the Grape River," which was likely a key inspiration to settlers in Monroe County, the birthplace of Michigan's first commercial wine industry.

Agritourism and World-Class Wines

Michigan's wine history is laden with tales of discovery, perseverance and passion for crafting wine from fruits that thrive in our soils. In *The History of Michigan Wines*, we document the state's wine history like never before. It's not a technical history; more so, it's a history that presents winemaking pioneers and their wines, which reflect our Great Lake State's unique characteristics and agricultural bounty.

Michigan's winemaking history is relatively young, compared to renowned regions of the Old World, though its history is just as fascinating. Our winemakers of today are writing their history and expanding our already rich heritage by producing world-class, award-winning wines. Equally exciting are the culinary destinations that showcase Michigan wines and foods produced from our agricultural bounty. Michigan wine country is a prime destination for reconnecting with the land.

Discover flavor that is uniquely Michigan. The wines reflect our Great Lakes, our place on earth and our winemakers' skills. Wine is grown from the ground; so when you think local foods, think local wines, both of which are rooted in and reflective of our Great Lake State and our rich, agricultural history. Read on to uncover Michigan's vibrant wine history and learn how the second most agriculturally diverse state and top tourism region has become a premier agritourism destination.

WINEMAKING PIONEERS

Mid-1800s to Early 1900s

Michigan's first commercial wine industry was ignited in Monroe County in the mid-1800s by savvy businessmen who planted vineyards and ventured into winemaking. Wine production was widespread in the state, yet Monroe County gained the reputation for quality wines produced by regional winemakers. The region produced half of the state's total wine through the late 1800s, shipping wines throughout the region and into markets like Chicago, New York and Philadelphia.

Flourishing grapevines along the southwest shore of Lake Michigan attracted a Welch's grape juice plant to Lawton. In turn, Welch's encouraged fruit growers to plant more vineyards to support the booming juice industry. Soon, Michigan was among the leading growers of grapes in the nation.

By 1883, however, grape rot had begun to seep into southeast Michigan and destroyed Monroe County's once healthy vineyards, triggering the demise of the region's wine industry. At the same time, the temperance movement was heating up across the nation. With the enactment of the Eighteenth Amendment, the National Prohibition Act of 1920, legal wine production in Michigan was stomped out.

MONROE COUNTY: MICHIGAN'S FIRST VIABLE WINE REGION

On July 14, 1817, following the War of 1812 and the 1813 River Raisin Battles, Governor Lewis Cass of the Michigan Territory established the District of Monroe County in recognition of President James Monroe, who had visited the area. When the Michigan Territory was admitted into the United States of America on January 26, 1837, as the twenty-sixth state of the union, Monroe was one of the largest towns in Michigan. Within a few decades, this region would become the birthplace of Michigan's commercial wine industry.

JOSEPH M. STERLING AND THE POINTE AUX PEAUX WINE COMPANY

On October 16, 1835, seventeen-year-old Joseph Marvin Sterling of Jefferson County, New York, arrived in Monroe on the steamer *Bradley* after stopping in Ohio to earn additional passage. Perhaps as Joseph traveled on Lake Erie, the combination of the sight of the grapevines on Kelleys Island and the wild grapevines flourishing along the Detroit River and the River Raisin influenced his future profession as winemaker. Joseph would be the first to plant a vineyard in the Monroe region for the commercial purpose of making wine.

Soon after Joseph's arrival, he became a prominent citizen involved in several businesses, one of which was a partnership with William A. Noble in warehousing. Joseph also built several private homes and public buildings, including the city hall, and served as mayor of Monroe from 1862 to 1863. Interestingly, he was offered the nomination to run for governor of Michigan on several occasions and declined.

In 1863, Joseph planted the state's first vineyard for the purposes of commercial winemaking in Monroe County, although the first vineyard in Monroe was planted in 1854 by J.C.W. Greening, owner of the River Raisin Valley Nursery. Joseph's vineyard was two and a half acres and was planted along with an apple orchard near the docks in Monroe. A few years later, he bought a thirty-acre parcel along the shores of Lake Erie in Frenchtown Township near Monroe for a summertime residence for his family. Incidentally, he bought the land for $2,012 from the son of the previous owner, Mr. Sancrainte, believed to be the first white settler in the area.

Successful vineyards on nearby islands inspired Joseph to plant a vineyard. He planted 2,050 vines of Concord, Delaware, Catawba, Ives Seedling and Norton's Virginia on twelve acres of the property.

A few years later, in 1868, commercial winemaking in Michigan commenced when Joseph established the Pointe Aux Peaux Wine Company with William Noble, Caleb Ives and Samuel P. Williams. The winery was named for the point of land that juts out into Lake Erie. Pointe Aux Peaux translates to "Point of Skins," which refers to the pelts and skins that Indians dried on the flat rocks along the lakeshore.

In 1870, a two-story winery was erected after three years of construction. It was built from limestone brought by vessel from Sandusky, Ohio. An air chamber left between the exterior stone wall and the interior brick wall enabled the winemakers to maintain year-round temperatures of roughly sixty degrees. The first floor was the wine cellar, and the second floor was used for pressing grapes and as a tasting room for visitors.

In 1871, the Pointe Aux Peaux winery processed sixty-nine thousand pounds of grapes and five thousand gallons of wine. According to Talcott E. Wing, a historian who wrote *History of Monroe County, Michigan* in 1890, "The

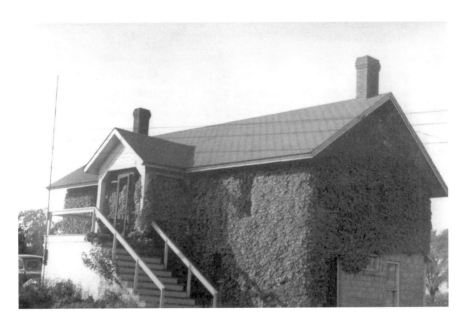

Michigan's first commercial winery, Pointe Aux Peaux Wine Company, built in 1868 in the Monroe region. *Courtesy of the Monroe County Historical Museum.*

wines gained a reputation for their purity and were extensively used for medicinal purposes as well as a beverage." Interestingly, Wing's son, Austin, was married to Joseph's daughter, Emma.

The winery's high-quality reputation quickly grew when the gentlemen of the Pointe Aux Peaux Wine Company entered their wines in the 1872 Michigan State Fair, achieving the first premium, a gold medal, and recognition for presenting the best collection of wines.

The following year, during the 1873 Michigan State Fair, William Beal of the Michigan Agricultural College and the State Pomological Society, along with several other committee members, visited several vineyards for examination. The committee awarded a gold medal to the Pointe Aux Peaux vineyard after it was noted as a perfect vineyard in all points of examination, exclaiming that it "had never seen any vineyard better laden with fruit or in better condition in any respect."

During the evaluation, one of the committee members asked Joseph if he thought it was wise to let his hogs run wild through the vineyards. Joseph credited the hogs for keeping insects and other rodents away from the vines, which allowed for the growth of great-quality fruit.

In an 1874 report by the State Pomological Society to the Michigan Horticultural Society, the committee praised Pointe Aux Peaux Wine Company, pronouncing

> *the Concord of 1871 as the best and most perfect. This was a white wine of a fine golden color, a delicious bouquet, a fair strength and a flavor that showed it had much of the full spirit of the soul of the grape. The Delaware of 1870 is a very delicate wine with much less bouquet and flavor, but is ripened by age, and so light to the taste that its fine body and strength is hardly appreciated or felt. As a wine for the sick it is probably unsurpassed.*

Joseph continued to be recognized as a savvy business leader in the community. In 1877, he served on the executive committee of the Michigan State Agricultural Society and was, notably, the chairman of the business committee for twelve years.

Pointe Aux Peaux Wine Company continued to thrive for a couple of decades until grape rot, in about 1883 and 1884, spread through the region deteriorating the vineyards. The vineyard was abandoned, yet the winery continued processing wine from the cellar and barrels for several more years.

More Wineries in the Monroe Region

After Joseph planted the first vineyard, Christopher Bruckner planted three hundred vines the subsequent year. Numerous others immediately followed, and vineyard acreage in the region quickly expanded.

One of these pioneers was Anton Weier, who emigrated from Wackerhiem, Rheim Hesse, Germany. He imported Concord grapes from New York and planted a small vineyard in 1884. By 1891, though, his company, Weier Wine Company, had a thirty-acre vineyard and a wine cellar with capacity to hold 140,000 gallons. He primarily used Catawba, Golden Concord, Delaware and American Claret for the wines produced by his winery. Before his death in 1907, Anton worked with his son, August, who learned winemaking from his father.

Also in 1865, Joseph Sedlaczek, who arrived from Munchengraetz, Bohemia, to Monroe in 1852, planted a four-acre vineyard and began experimenting as a wine grower. By 1872, he was producing nearly fifteen thousand gallons of wine each year. The business was largely wholesale, consisting of shipments to New York and Chicago.

Joseph eventually partnered with Joseph Weier (no relation to Anton Weier), who arrived in Monroe in 1849 and planted a vineyard in 1865. Eventually, he was producing two thousand to five thousand gallons of wine and sending wine to Philadelphia and New York City. At some point, the Monroe Wine Company was formed with Joseph Weier as president and Joseph Sedlaczek as superintendent. Incidentally, Joseph Weier served as representative of Monroe County from 1869 to 1870.

John Kressbach, a renowned winemaker in the region, was in charge of the Detroit Wine Company, headquartered in Monroe, from 1868 until his death in 1888. The winery had fourteen acres of vines, planted around the same time, adjacent to the city of Monroe.

By 1867, more than fifty acres of vines had been planted in the region, and the acreage was expected to double in ensuing years. By 1873, more than twenty vineyards on nearly two hundred acres were producing 600,000 pounds of grapes. The grape varieties were Concord, Catawba, Delaware, Ives Seedling, Norton's Virginia and Hartford Prolific, as well as a few other varieties that were occasionally added for experimental purposes.

In 1873, another notable settler of the area was George W. Bruckner, who established Lotus Island Vineyard, consisting of five acres of Concord and Catawba vines. A year later, Snake Island was renamed to Bruckner's Lotus

Island as a tribute to the winemaker. Another island nearby was owned by Bruckner and E.J. Boyd, who grew mostly Concord and smaller amounts of Catawba and Delaware grapes.

In 1880, most of the Monroe vineyards were destroyed by a very severe hailstorm that hit on July 18. Grapes were bought from growers from other regions at an average of two cents per pound.

By 1883, before the grape rot started to set in, Monroe County had 309 acres of vines; 184,673 pounds of grapes were sold, and 12,335 gallons of wine were made. Monroe's wine industry was booming and earning praise for its finely produced wines.

PLANTINGS BEYOND THE MONROE REGION

At the same time that Monroe's wine industry was established, vineyard plantings in Michigan's other remote regions were cropping up. It was common for European settlers to plant private vineyards to continue long-standing Old World family traditions of making wine for personal enjoyment.

By 1871, nearly twenty-five thousand vines had been planted in the state. By 1884, 24,685 gallons of wine were produced in Michigan. Of the 3,228 acres of vineyards, 1,550,702 pounds of grapes were sold. Notably, half of the wine production was in Monroe County. Beyond Monroe, grape plantings were scattered throughout the state.

In Westphalia, in Clinton County, Reverend Father Goedetz, a pastor of the Catholic Church, planted grapes in 1850. Apparently, church parishioners followed his lead, and it wasn't long before nearly every farm in the area had grapevines. By 1887, wine was being produced in considerable quantities and profits were good.

In 1862, Jonathon G. Ramsdell, a circuit court judge in Grand Traverse County, gained a reputation for testing and showcasing fruit varietals. A two-and-a-half-acre vineyard on Old Mission Peninsula overlooking Grand Traverse Bay was graced with Iona, Wilder, Delaware, Concord and Agawam grape varieties.

Jonathon stated that Iona was worth fifteen cents a pound for the manufacturing of wine, though he shared:

I have abandoned grape culture, and ought to have ripped out my vines last year, but was too tender-hearted. The truth is, the little insects known as thripes have met me and I am theirs…The vineyard that has been my pride will be given up and I shall abandon the business.

Unfortunately, his vineyard did not survive, and it wasn't until a century later that vineyards were planted for commercial wine production in northern Michigan.

In 1870, George Parmalee of Old Mission Peninsula (who at one point was an appointee of the Michigan State Horticultural Society) encouraged farmers to plant different fruit varietals. This prompted fruit grower Edward Bradfield to experiment with every grape variety grown in the country. In 1873, he planted thirty-eight varieties in Ada in Kent County and determined that Iona was best for making wine.

In 1884, in Gratiot County, 47 acres of vineyards were planted, and 3,294 gallons of wine were produced. To the east, Bay County had 34 acres of vines planted, which generated 2,349 gallons of wine. More than 833 acres of grapevines were producing grapes in Berrien County, though only 677 gallons of wine were recorded. Nearly 500,000 pounds of grapes were sold.

ALONG THE SHORES OF LAKE MICHIGAN: THE GREAT FRUIT BELT

In the 1800s, indigenous and cultivated fruits were flourishing in Michigan, nurtured by European settlers and Native Americans. In southwest Michigan, fresh fruit from the region was shipped from Benton Harbor to Chicago as early as 1839 for the commercial market.

Lake Michigan's prevailing westerly winds create unique growing conditions. The massive freshwater lake moderates seasonal temperatures, cooling the air in the summer and warming the air in the fall. This is called lake effect. This buffer on the climate extends the warmer growing season for regions located near the state's west coast, allowing fruit to flourish as it does in more southern climates, resulting in a fruit belt.

In 1856, in the fruit belt region of Van Buren County, A.B. Jones bought a small farm near Paw Paw Station, a depot built where an Indian trail and the railroad intersected (now Lawton). A.B. planted a few grapevines, possibly Delawares, on his farm and eventually sent a few packages of grapes to Lansing, where he received twelve to fifteen cents a pound and cleared about forty dollars. This prompted him to plant several hundred vines in 1868 and

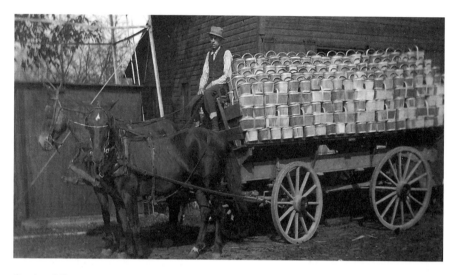

Carting full grape baskets from the Paw Paw area vineyards to a processing plant in the 1800s. *Courtesy of St. Julian Wine Company.*

name his farm Pioneer Vineyards. The grape growing and supply business made him a prosperous gentleman of the time.

In 1870, the Kalamazoo and South Haven Railroad was in place, followed a year later by the Chicago and Michigan Lake Shore Railroad. Michigan's southern forests provided lumber to rebuild Chicago after the devastating fire of 1871. The cleared land was planted with fruit trees, and the railway, originally built to transport lumber, was also a shipping means for fruit into the bustling Chicago market.

By 1880, more than two thousand acres of vines were thriving in the region. Of course, A.B. had no idea that his vineyard planting would stimulate Michigan's oldest, continuously operating wine industry. The region's flourishing fruit farms attracted Welch's to this region in 1919, a pivotal milestone in Michigan's vineyard history. As Monroe's wine region essentially ceased during Prohibition, Van Buren County's vineyards thrived, supplying its bountiful baskets of grapes to Welch's for grape juice production. Southwest Michigan farmland was thriving with Concord and Niagara grapevines, while additional varieties were being evaluated for their ability to withstand Michigan's cold climate and four seasons.

The State's First Fruit-Testing Farm

On March 31, 1849, the Michigan State Agricultural Society was established through the state legislature for the purpose of promoting the improvement of agriculture in the state. Incidentally, the state's first state fair was held in Detroit the same year. Within six years, by 1855, Michigan Agricultural College (now Michigan State University) had opened in East Lansing.

In 1883, horticulture became an independent department at the college. Agricultural research in the state was on the rise under the direction of Liberty Hyde Bailey Jr., who became the department chair in 1885. The importance of research was also recognized nationally with the Hatch Act of 1887, which provided funds through federal land grants to set up experimental agricultural stations for colleges established within the Morrill Act (often referred to as the Land Grant Act).

Michigan's first experiment station under the act was established in South Haven in 1889 on the farm of Theodatus Timothy Lyon. He had extensive plantings of various fruit cultivars, including eighty-seven varieties of grapes. He also served as president of the State Pomological Society of Michigan and was active in the Michigan State Horticultural Society. Interestingly, someone drew a crayon portrait of Theodatus and presented it to him at a meeting. It is stated that the drawing was sent to permanently hang in the state capitol.

Incidentally, Theodatus, along with Joseph M. Sterling and S.O. Knapp, were identified as fruit experts and appointed to a committee by Governor John Bagley to showcase the state's finest fruits in Chicago.

The Demise of the Monroe Wine Industry

In 1891, Joseph M. Sterling passed away from pneumonia at age seventy-three. Within the year, the wife or daughter of his winery partner, Samuel P. Williams, discarded the remaining wine, as she was active in the temperance movement. The families were forced to close the wine business.

The property stayed in the family for years, remaining a favorite summertime destination through the 1940s. The value of this spectacular land along Lake Erie increased, and development ensued on the prime real estate that was once home to Michigan's burgeoning wine industry.

After the demise of the winery, Pointe Aux Peaux's two-story building was converted to a house for the caretakers. Soon after, the old winery building earned the name the "Stone House." Notably, the Stone House still stands today and is the oldest winery building in the state of Michigan. Also of note, Gerald Burrer bought the property in 1946. Upon his passing, his son, Bill Burrer, sold the property, stipulating that the new buyer preserve the winery building for its historical value to the area. Today, the Stone House is connected seamlessly to a modern lake house overlooking Lake Erie.

In 1885, a logbook was started at the cottage built in front of the Pointe Aux Peaux winery building. The first entry was on July 1, 1885, and stated, "The buildings, vineyard and grounds looked nicely." A copy of this logbook is available at the Monroe County Historical Museum.

Due to the grape rot of the late 1800s, the deaths of the pioneering winemakers and the temperance movement, Monroe's once-booming wine region was in decline. At the same time, the temperance movement was heating up across the country.

Temperance Movement on the Rise

Michigan's first active temperance movement occurred long before the emergence of the National Prohibition Act of the early 1900s. Issues against alcohol arose from the time of the very first settlements in Michigan, when white traders were accused of taking advantage of Native Americans by getting them drunk for better trade arrangements for furs and other items. In 1832, an act was established in Michigan that forbade the sale of intoxicants to the natives or the introduction of liquor into Native American communities.

During the early 1800s, it was common to consume alcohol on a regular basis. This was a time before soda pop, juice and public water systems, and even the lack of refrigeration made milk more of a premium beverage. Alcohol was often consumed during lunch and work breaks, and public intoxication was common. It was around this time that the temperance movement began heating up across the country.

The first organized temperance group in Michigan was the Detroit Society for the Suppression of Intemperance, established on February 19, 1830. General Charles Larned, who served in both the Revolutionary War and the War of 1812, was the first president of the society. In 1832, it was renamed to the Detroit Temperance Society, and it expanded statewide the following year, procuring the new name of Michigan Temperance Society.

On national and political levels, General Lewis Cass, former governor of the Michigan Territory from 1813 to 1831, twice a member of the cabinet of the United States and current secretary of war, was one of Michigan's most notable early leaders in the movement. When he entered the temperance movement, he proclaimed that he had always been a "cold-water man."

In 1832, the general issued an order

> *forbidding the introduction of ardent spirits into any fort, camp, or garrison in the United States, and prohibiting their sale by any sutler to the troops. As a substitute for the ardent spirits issued previously, and for the commutation in money prescribed thereby, eight pounds of sugar and four pounds of coffee will be allowed to every one hundred rations.*

After the Congressional Temperance Society was rejuvenated in 1842, General Cass became the first president of the society. The society was driven to move the nation toward total abstinence from alcohol and played an important political role in the movement for several decades.

Due to strong leadership and willful force, prohibition laws were eventually implemented in Michigan, though the process experienced several adversities before a sound prohibition was established. In 1851, the state constitution added a clause banning alcohol as follows: "The legislature shall not pass any act authorizing the grant of license for the sale of ardent spirits or other intoxicating liquors." However, the language forgot to outlaw the sale of alcohol by individuals and companies without a license and was, therefore, not effective.

Two years later, in 1853, Michigan adopted the Maine Law, a prohibition law originating in Maine in 1851 that was quickly adopted by twelve additional states. Within a year, the State Supreme Court had deemed the law unconstitutional due to defects in the law. Finally, the following year, nearly seventy years before the Eighteenth Amendment, a solid prohibition was in effect, although it was amended in 1857 to allow wine, beer and cider consumption, much to the frustration of Michigan's temperance leaders. This early prohibition in Michigan remained vital for more than twenty years, although the ban was rarely enforced.

Soon, women became the major force of the temperance movement. Married women were dependent on their husbands to financially provide for their families. Husbands who frequently drank might be unable to work, spend too much money and cheat on their wives or become abusive to or abandon their families. Many women blamed alcohol for these actions. Divorce was not a common or acceptable option at the time.

Women crusaders teamed up across the nation to close down saloons by praying and singing inside until the owner agreed to close. Any owner who did not immediately close down was visited a second time by the committee, accompanied by legal enforcement authorities. It was clear, though, by 1875 that Michigan's early prohibition was not working, and the banning of alcohol was repealed.

Around the same time, the Women's National Christian Temperance Union of Michigan, established in Adrian before spreading throughout the state, continued to vocally object to the sins of alcohol. The union's vice-president, Jane M. Geddes, expressed her thoughts about the start of the earlier women's crusade:

> We had at that time a prohibitory law, which had been standing on the statute book some eighteen or nineteen years, and under it all the saloons and drinking places in Adrian were shut up so closely that for six weeks there was no open drinking in town. During those six weeks the sum of fifty dollars covered all the expense of the criminal business of the city.

Jane quickly gained notoriety as Michigan's leader of the new women's temperance movement.

On November 24, 1876, Jane and her husband, Judge Norman Geddes, hosted Dr. Henry A. Reynolds in Adrian. The Reynolds reform movement, which grew throughout Michigan, started in Adrian and then expanded into Tecumseh, Hillsdale, Coldwater and Monroe before reaching additional cities. According to an author of this era, W.H. Daniels, "This was the first uprising of the drunkards themselves in favor of total abstinence that had ever been seen in those parts."

The following year in Lansing, a Reform Club was organized, enrolling "drinking men over a thousand" in a city with only 1,850 voters. At one of the meetings, Dr. Reynolds proclaimed:

> The first Red Ribbon worn in Congress will go into the House of Representatives on the coat of Edwin Willetts of Monroe, Michigan. You want to know why we have a Red Ribbon? Well, I will tell you. A few

years ago a lot of good, big-hearted, whole-souled fellows, who had been in the habit of drinking, got together and resolved that they would rather wear a Red Ribbon than a red nose…the ribbon is tied in a knot, you see, for the reason that no man would like to go into a saloon and ask for a drink with that badge on; and while he was stopping to untie it the Lord would come in, and cast the devil of appetite out of him, and save him.

The force of these group leaders and others led Michigan into a second state of prohibition, quickly followed by prohibition on a national level.

A DRY STATE, A DRY COUNTRY

By 1911, nearly half of Michigan's eighty-three counties had adopted dry ordinances. Five years later, in 1916, the Michigan Constitution passed the Prohibition Amendment. The state legislature also implemented the Damon Act, which prohibited liquor from entering Michigan from other states and foreign countries, although on February 18, 1919, the Michigan Supreme Court ruled the Damon Act unconstitutional.

By 1918, the temperance movement had prevailed, and Michigan banned alcohol on May 1, 1918—a year and a half before the Eighteenth Amendment banned alcohol in all states in the union. On January 16, 1920, the United States Constitution prohibited the manufacture, sale, transport, import and export of alcoholic beverages on a national level. The rollicking era of Prohibition had arrived.

PROHIBITION AND WINE

1918 to 1933

Prohibition in Michigan was an era of innovative bootlegging, federal raids of blind pigs and the establishment of a dynamic wine industry. Remarkably, the ban on alcohol spurred a prosperous new industry in Detroit. Rather than aid in tempering the consumption of alcohol, the act triggered the illegal trafficking of alcohol and resulted in an era of speakeasies, blind pigs and private clubs, where gambling, racketeering and murder were commonplace for the next thirteen years.

In Detroit, it was almost as if Prohibition had never happened, a situation that was devastating to leaders of the temperance groups and prohibition advocates. One notable advocate was Henry Ford, of the Ford Motor Company, who offered his autoworkers a pay of five dollars a day—a substantially high wage at the time—while requiring abstinence from alcohol. To his frustrations and others', prohibition was not taken very seriously in Michigan, and within ten years, illegal liquor would generate $215 million in revenue in Detroit, second only to the automobile industry. It was for this reason, perhaps, that in Detroit, the Roaring Twenties were often referred to as the "Prospering Twenties."

THE DETROIT RIVER:
BIG BUSINESS FOR BOOTLEGGERS

In Detroit, most people did not take the ban on alcohol seriously. According to longtime reporter and editor Malcolm Bingay, "It was absolutely impossible to get a drink in Detroit, unless you walked ten feet and told the busy bartender what you wanted in a voice loud enough for him to hear you above the uproar."

The narrow width of the Detroit River, which is less than a mile wide in some sections, was an open invitation to enterprising businessmen, spawning the rumrunning of liquor, beer and wine across the channel between Ontario, Canada, and Michigan. Interestingly, prohibition was also established in Ontario at the time, though wineries using native Canadian grapes were exempt, and the production of beer and liquor to be distributed to wet territories was legal. Not surprisingly, this production rarely made it to its proclaimed destinations.

The abundant islands in the thirty-two-mile Detroit River provided ample coverage for moving contraband across the river into the United States. The narrow strip of water between countries offered clever means for transportation throughout the seasons. An underwater cable system moved contraband along the bottom of the river. Speedboats traversed from shore to shore in roughly four minutes. Fishing boats with fold-up motors moved stealthily across the water. Sleds and convoys of automobiles crossed over the ice when the river froze during winter.

Most people, even women and children, took part in carrying illegal booze across the river for personal use, though bootlegging for profit was largely controlled by the infamous Purple Gang, a vicious group of Jewish immigrant gangsters, and the Italian Mafia. Crime in Detroit was explosive during this era, justifying 27 percent of the entire federal enforcement budget allotted for the Detroit area alone.

The combined region of the Detroit River, Lake St. Clair and the St. Clair River earned the nickname "the Detroit-Windsor funnel" for the massive amount of alcohol transported across these waterways. Roughly 75 percent of all contraband entered the United States via the Detroit River.

Most of the transported alcohol was hard liquor and beer. Wine was limited to small quantities of French wines and Champagne and wine produced by a few vintners of Canada. However, the consumption of wine increased during Prohibition. Home wine production was legal in small quantities, with low alcohol content and for personal consumption. Oftentimes, wine was crafted from grapes creatively packaged by California growers or from grapes purchased from Detroit's Eastern Market after being harvested and transported from the vineyards of southwest Michigan.

SOUTHWEST VINEYARDS FLOURISH

Vineyards along Michigan's southwest coast were thriving at the commencement of Prohibition and even experienced major expansion during the national ban on alcohol. The region experienced a high demand for grapes for home wine production and, more significantly, for grape juice production. The large quantity and high quality of Concord, Niagara and

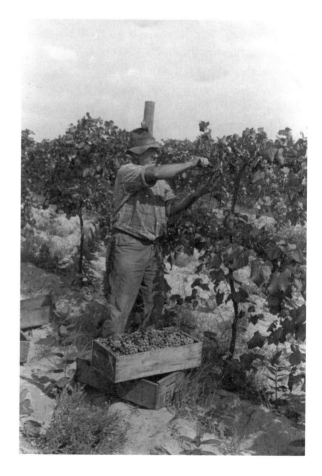

Farmer Giuseppe Ceru on the family farm on Fourth Street in Kalamazoo. *Courtesy of Vander Beek and Turan families.*

other grape varietals growing in the area attracted a Welch's plant in Lawton in 1919.

Years earlier, in 1869, Dr. Thomas Bramwell Welch and his son, Charles, applied pasteurization to Concord grape juice, launching the advent of the processed grape juice industry. A temperance advocate, Dr. Welch crafted unfermented wine to use during church communion services in Vineland, New Jersey. Upon the opening of the Michigan plant, Welch encouraged even more plantings of vineyards in the region.

In addition to supplying grapes to Welch's, the region's growers sent grapes to markets such as Detroit's Eastern Market and into the Chicago market via the railroad.

HOME WINE AND BREW PRODUCTION

Widespread home winemaking and brewing prevailed during Prohibition. Invariably, Section 29, Title II, of the Volstead Act created a loophole by not clearly defining "intoxicating" or "fruit juices." The section allowed a person to manufacture "non-intoxicating cider and fruit juice exclusively for home use," as long as it was not sold or delivered except to "persons having permits to manufacture vinegar." Home production of wine and brews was supported by the establishment of sugarhouses that provided supplies. The sugarhouses became the fronts for big bootlegging businesses, as corn sugar does not generate odor or ash when brewed—ultimate attributes for the illegal production of mass quantities of alcohol. This caused a boom in corn sugar production.

Due to Section 29, backyard vineyards dotted Michigan's rolling landscape throughout this era. Families continued Old World traditions, growing grapevines, making wines and consuming them with friends and family.

Those who were unable to maintain vineyards purchased grapes grown within the state or one of the famous grape bricks from California. Grape bricks were dehydrated grapes formed into bricks and sold for so-called homemade juice making. The instructions stated to dissolve the brick in water, add sugar to taste and consume within five days, otherwise it may ferment and become wine.

Remarkably, Section 29 became the grounds on which a small mining town in Michigan's Upper Peninsula defied the United States government

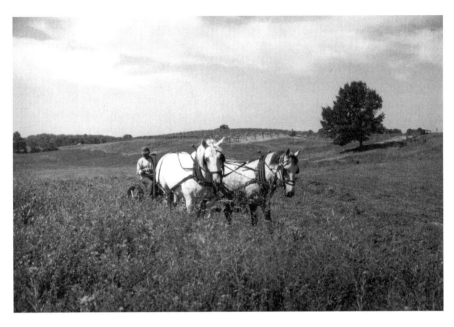

Plowing the family farm and vineyards in the 1920s. *Courtesy of Vander Beek and Turan families.*

only one month after the Volstead Act was adopted. Michigan garnered national headlines for a federal raid, which surprisingly took place more than five hundred miles northwest of the Detroit River region.

IRON RIVER REBELLION

In the 1800s, Europeans flocked to Michigan's Upper Peninsula after the discovery of iron ore and copper. The mining industry exploded. For the next eighty years, 175 million tons of iron ore were shipped out of Iron County. Notably, a large colony of Italians settled in the small town of Iron River in the county, just a few miles from the Wisconsin border, to work the mines. Naturally, the Italians resumed home winemaking, a family tradition in Europe.

In 1914, prominent Italian merchant John Scalcucci bought a ten-year-old building in proximity to the iron ore being mined by Italian workers. With his brothers, Stephen and Joseph Scalcucci, John opened a grocery store to cater to the miners and their families. The Scalcucci family handcrafted wine in the store basement, where they pressed the grapes.

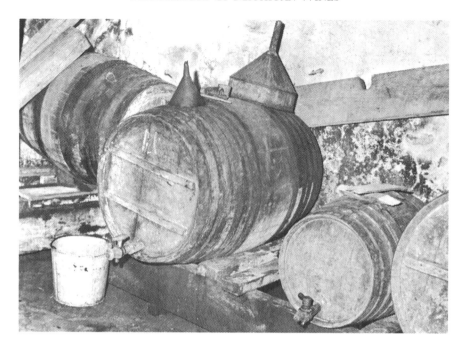

Barrels used by the Scalcuccis for winemaking in the 1800s. *Courtesy of Iron County Historical Museum.*

The Chianti-style wine was a popular drink of the region, preferred over water and sold alongside other grocery staples. As was commonly stated, "The miners know the quality of the wine…They don't know the quality of the water." This, of course, was before the advent of public water systems.

The Scalcucci wine was likely made with Zinfandel or Alicante Bouschet, a vinifera grape, which was commonly used for wine production during Prohibition. Grapes were grown in California and then shipped by railroad in ventilated cattle cars to the East Coast. Zinfandel does not travel well; however, Alicante Bouschet, due to its thick skin, transports quite well and is less susceptible to grape rot. During this time, as many as ten to twelve carloads of grapes were ordered for wine production in this region.

Within a month of the instatement of Prohibition, on Valentine's Day, state constabulary officers raided the Scalcucci grocery store and seized eight and a half barrels of homemade wine. The brothers had made an abundance of wine due to a large crop of grapes that arrived by rail and could not be sold. Immediately, state's attorney Martin McDonough demanded that the wine be returned to the Scalcuccis since the officers did not have a search warrant to raid the Scalcucci home, which was situated on the second floor above the grocery store. Martin asked the court to dismiss this case against the Scalcuccis, noting that home wine production was allowed under Section 29.

A disgruntled constabulary member notified Leo J. Grove, a Marquette-based federal prohibition supervisor. On February 19, Leo led a handful of state constables to Iron River and confiscated the wine barrels.

Once again, Martin demanded that the wine be returned to the Scalcuccis after Leo failed to show a search warrant. Martin then told the brothers, "If federal authorities attempt to remove the wine again, open fire on them."

These incidents prompted Leo to contact Chicago-based Major A.V. Dalrymple, chief prohibition enforcement officer for the central western states. Grove informed the officer about the revolt in Iron River. The major requested a search warrant from Marquette-based federal prohibition commissioner H.B. Hatch for a third raid on Iron River. In turn, the commissioner directed him to the Grand Rapids district attorney's office. However, district attorney Myron Walker did not feel he had enough facts to issue a warrant.

Regardless, the major proclaimed with much zeal, "Iron County is in open rebellion against prohibition," and he raced to Iron River via the railroad to arrest state's attorney Martin McDonough, the chief of police, five deputy sheriffs and the Scalcucci brothers.

On this same morning, February 23, the news of the impending raid and the major's plans to make arrests was broadcast across the United States with such headlines as "Whisky Rebellion; U.S. Defied in Michigan" and "Dry Force Invades Michigan."

Reporters beat the major to Iron River and quickly connected with Martin, who vocally supported the Scalcucci brothers and their leadership in the community, as well as the large foreign worker base, stating, "These foreigners always have their grape presses and their homemade wine. They drink this in preference to water. They carry it to their work in their dinner pails and they won't work without it."

On February 24, the major and state constabulary agents from Negaunee raced by sled to Iron River. Reports of the armed invasion descending on Iron River triggered the dumping of thousands of gallons of wine by Iron River residents; however, thousands more were salvaged, as wine was hauled by ox sled and automobile into the woods, mine shafts and tunnels.

When the major arrived in Iron River, Martin greeted him and prepared to serve a warrant for his arrest for "publications of false and malicious stories" about Martin and Iron County. The major conceded for the moment and retired to the Iron Inn for the evening.

The next morning, on February 25, the major and his men arrived with six hundred rounds of ammunition and raided the locked basement of the parish priest's home, where Martin had moved the Scalcucci wine for safekeeping. The marshals rolled the barrels out into the alley between St. Agnes Church and the school, broke open the barrels and dumped the wine in the snow. They then encouraged the swarm of newspaper reporters who had flocked to Iron River to take photographs of the United States government taking Prohibition seriously.

Many Chicago newspapers, including the *Chicago Tribune, Chicago Daily News, Chicago Daily Journal* and the *Chicago Herald and Examiner* captured the event in headlines and photographs. Notably, a reporter for the *Pathé News* gave fifty cents to Necktie Sensiba, a school student, to scoop up the wine-flavored pink snow and eat it like a snow cone. This image was subsequently shown on silent newsreels throughout the nation.

Finally, on the afternoon of February 25, a ceasefire was reached after the major was ordered by the national prohibition commissioner via telegraph

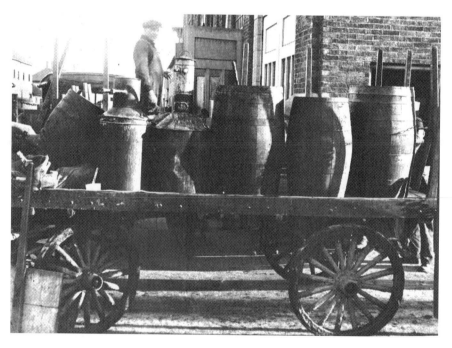

A dray, owned by Iron County resident John Singler, loaded with confiscated barrels and stills in 1920, shortly after the Iron River Rebellion. *Courtesy of Iron County Historical Museum.*

to compromise with Martin to end the debacle. The farce had created a major rift between the department of justice and the department of internal revenue. The infamous Iron River Rebellion ended with the major returning to Chicago the following day and, within the year, resigning from his post.

Nationwide reports were issued of Martin's heroic defiance and stand in the rebellion. On February 28, the State of Michigan dropped its investigation into the Iron River Rebellion, and Martin was hailed as a hero. The *Chicago Tribune* reported at the end, "And tonight the old 'home brew' is being dug up again from its hiding places in the hill."

Today, the abandoned building that once harbored the Scalcucci grocery store and the making of the infamous wine is protected by the Michigan State Preservation Office and registered as one of the state's historic sites. An annual festival, the Rum Rebellion Heritage Days, honors this dynamic event in the region's past with four days of family activities, including skits of the historic event and parade awards with such names as the McDonough Award.

Wine Goes Down the Drain During Raid

Like the Scalcuccis, families throughout Michigan continued to make wine during Prohibition. Seventy miles north of Iron River, in Rockland, the Gagnon family fermented anything they could get their hands on, including wild dandelions and beets. They often made wine from the bounty of native grapes growing in the area and spiked it with moonshine to perk it up. Drinks were sold in the H&E Gagnon Bros. Sample Room, the Gagnons' blind pig, one of forty in the copper mining town of five thousand people.

The business, run by brothers Henry and Elias Gagnon, flourished until Elias Gagnon was arrested for selling moonshine. Apparently, a disgruntled Rockland resident reported the illegal actions to federal officers because the Gagnons were receiving better cuts of meat from the local butcher during a time of meat rationing. The night before the raid, Henry's eldest son, Lynn Henry Gagnon, took off for Chicago, where he hid for a few years. During the raid, Henry's nine-year-old twins, Ed and Katherine, dumped a massive amount of wine down the bathtub to avoid detection. Unfortunately, the authorities located moonshine beneath the ground of a chicken coop, and Elias spent eighteen months in Leavenworth.

Across the street was another blind pig run by brothers Dud and John Schmaus. They managed their booze business from a cigar box to facilitate a fast getaway with the money in the event that things turned bad quickly. Their widowed mother, Mary, supplied wine and moonshine for the business as a means of raising her eight sons and two daughters. Mary's wines gained a reputation for "knocking your socks off." She always had a huge crock of wine fermenting behind the kitchen stove, while she kept her still in the outhouse up by the old Minnesota Mine. Customers loved the wine, though they bluntly stated that the moonshine was awful. Still, it always sold.

Today, wild grapevines still flourish in Rockland near the coast of Lake Superior. The old Sample Room, now called Henry's Inn, is still owned by the Gagnon family, and the Schmaus building later became the Pantti building.

WINERIES GET STARTED DURING PROHIBITION

Wine production continued to be a hopping business in the Upper Peninsula, while bootlegging along the Detroit River raged on. Notably, three Michigan winemakers—Mariano Meconi, Major (Morris) R. Twomey and Angelo Spinazze started in Ontario, Canada, before leading Michigan's post-Prohibition wine industry.

Mariano Meconi and Border City Wine Cellars

In 1909, Mariano Meconi emigrated from Faleria in the province of Viterbo, Italy, at age thirteen to Windsor, Ontario, Canada, with his two brothers. They settled in the Windsor region, home to a large base of Italian immigrants.

At age twenty-six, Mariano established Border City Wine Cellars, unknowingly launching the advent of his family's longstanding wine history in North America. In Windsor, he initially worked at the Studebaker auto factory and for the railroad, most likely the Canadian Pacific Railway or Great Western Railway. The railway provided transportation for lugging Canadian labrusca grapes from Essex County to Windsor to support his winemaking business. Using native grapes enabled Mariano to operate a winery during Ontario's Prohibition years.

Prohibition in the United States inspired the entrepreneur to be creative in distributing his wines across the Detroit River. After all, Detroit was home to sixteen thousand to twenty-five thousand blind pigs and speakeasies. Family lore says that Mariano's wines and whiskey traversed the Detroit River in a number of ways, including by boat using a collapsible motor.

A 1929 Everroot "fold light" motor was used for stealth crossings of the Detroit River to take the contraband into Detroit. The motor attached to a small outrigger boat. Once safely across the river, the transporters detached the motor, folded it up and hid it for later retrieval.

In the late 1920s, it was believed that Mariano was either a partner of or collected money for Joseph Kennedy in the sale of whiskey in the Detroit/ Windsor and the Port Huron/Sarnia areas under the name of Essex Import and Export Company. This partnership further enabled the winemaker to grow his business.

On Monday, December 5, 1932, Mariano's wine facility in Windsor, Ontario, was destroyed by a fire caused by a boiler explosion. Mariano continued to make wine and relocated his winery, now called Meconi Wine Company, to Detroit after Prohibition was repealed.

Maurice (Morris) R. Twomey, Angelo Spinazze and the Windsor Wine Company

While Mariano was ramping up his wine business, another future Michigan vintner was successfully managing his winery in Ontario. Wealthy Canadian Maurice (Morris) R. Twomey was a highly successful businessman and landowner. For seven years, Morris owned Windsor Wine Company in Walkerville, Ontario.

In 1927, Morris hired Angelo Spinazze to be a jack-of-all-trades. Angelo had immigrated to Canada from Colle Umberto in the province of Treviso in northern Italy. Angelo had lived on his family's small vineyard in Italy and, in junior high, studied at the school of enology and viticulture in Conegliano. His father produced much sought-after wines that were sold to local taverns and inns. In 1926, at age seventeen, Angelo immigrated to Windsor through Halifax, following his brothers to North America. He took a job with the Windsor Wine Company, where his brother Dominic worked.

Angelo did many odd jobs for Morris, including winemaking for Windsor Wine Company. He also acted as Morris's chauffeur, often driving him to cheer on the Detroit Tigers at Bennett Park, where he witnessed the legendary Babe Ruth of the New York Yankees play against the Tigers. Angelo also drove Morris to the high-rolling Book Cadillac Hotel in Detroit, which opened in 1924.

Angelo quickly earned Morris's respect during their years working together. Morris later recommended Angelo to the owners of the Detroit-based Bronte Champagne and Wines Company for the position of head winemaker. In the meantime, though, there was money to be made during Prohibition.

During this era, it was common practice to relabel goods to generate more revenue. High-end Piper-Heidsieck Champagne labels were placed on the less expensive Windsor Wine Company bottles to sell at a higher profit in Detroit. Often, Angelo was instructed to drop the Champagne off on the docks for covert transporting across the Detroit River. He never stuck around after the drop, though; instead, he quickly headed back to the winery to avoid any trouble.

As Prohibition came to an end in Michigan, the business-savvy Morris began massive renovations of an eighty-three-thousand-square-foot electrical powerhouse of the Detroit United Railway. In the fall of 1932, he converted the building to his new wine facility.

Interestingly, Morris relocated his winery to Farmington the same month that prohibition was repealed in Michigan and eight months before the national repeal. The move across the Detroit River prompted a name change. His new La Salle Wines and Champagne Company immediately had the capacity to produce 1,000,000 gallons of wine each year.

THE END OF PROHIBITION

It was apparent to most that Prohibition was a substantial failure. On February 20, 1933, the Twenty-first Amendment repealing Prohibition was proposed by Congress. Michigan was the first state to ratify the proposal on April 10, 1933. Thirty-six states were needed to ratify the amendment nationally. Prohibition officially ended on December 5, 1933, when Utah became the thirty-sixth state to ratify the proposal. Alcohol was legal again after thirteen years.

Although the state and national prohibition laws were repealed, several of Michigan's communities remained dry for years. In fact, the last community to repeal its prohibition laws was Hudsonville in Ottawa County, which removed its dry law as recently as November 2007. The law was reversed in hopes of stimulating economic growth in the community, an ironic move since some temperance advocates originally argued that prohibiting saloons and alcohol would improve business productivity.

The leadership of Mariano Meconi and Morris Twomey immediately following the repeal of Prohibition combined with the opening of several additional wineries reignited Michigan's wine industry. A new winemaking era had begun.

POST-PROHIBITION

Boom of the 1930s to 1950s

National demand for wine was high following the repeal of Prohibition in 1933. Even First Lady Eleanor Roosevelt immediately started serving American wines at the White House. These were the first wines in the White House since 1877, when First Lady Lucy Webb Hayes refused to serve alcohol, eventually garnering the nickname "Lemonade Lucy" for her active role in the temperance movement.

In Michigan, the lift on the ban of alcohol launched a dynamic era for the state's commercial wine industry. Within days of the repeal, at least two wineries relocated from Canada, and several wineries opened. Large-production winemaking facilities were immediately established to meet the demand of American wine drinkers.

Michigan's vintners had no problem finding ample fruit to produce their wines. A bounty of grapevines was flourishing in southwest Michigan after surviving Prohibition by supplying grapes to Welch's grape juice company. And the price of grapes was at an all-time low due to the Great Depression. The multitude of Concords, the most popular grape varietal used to produce these early wines, hit rock bottom at only ten dollars a ton.

The surplus of grapes at low prices, high-volume production facilities and demand for wine set the stage for a prosperous industry. Michigan's commercial wine industry was instantly rekindled.

Within only two years, nine wineries in Michigan were producing 350,000 gallons of wine, and annual production continued to grow substantially.

Soon, however, Michigan's wine production exceeded its demand, since wines produced with Concord grapes had a "foxy" taste and were not competing well with wines produced from other states, such as California and New York. A new law of 1937 levied a higher tax on out-of-state wines than on Michigan wines, and the state's sales increased dramatically over the next few decades.

Of the nine wineries, six were established in the Detroit region to be close to consumers. One of these first vintners was Major Maurice (Morris) R. Twomey. During a 1943 newspaper interview, Morris stated:

> *The largest consumption of wines in America is found among those of foreign birth or extraction. Authoritative sources state that the population of greater Detroit alone includes over 755,000 persons either foreign born or with at least one parent foreign born. According to the department of commerce figures, the Michigan market for wines in normal times is estimated at 4,000,000 gallons annually.*

It's not surprising that Morris, with his inherent business sense, opened a powerhouse winemaking facility that quickly became the third largest winery in the nation.

LA SALLE WINES AND CHAMPAGNE

From the start, Morris's vision for his Michigan winery was substantial. Several months before Prohibition ended, he laid the foundation for the state's largest-ever producing winery by renovating an eighty-three thousand square-foot building in Farmington into a massive wine production facility. On April 10, 1933, Morris relocated his Ontario-based Windsor Wine Company to the renovated facility and established La Salle Wines and Champagne.

During renovations, several unique features were installed to create a facility large enough to handle a production capacity of 1,000,000 gallons of wine. A third floor was added on top of the building to house crushing vats. The crushed grapes then went to the second floor to the fermentation tanks, which were perhaps the most unique feature of the winery. Concrete was poured to create vats that were then lined with glass. Each of the twenty fermentation tanks held about 6,000 gallons of wine. Once the wine was fermented, it was pumped into storage tanks on the ground floor. The original ground floor had been lowered to host twenty large oak aging casks holding about 4,000 gallons of wine each.

Morris recruited Otto Kuhm, who was highly regarded in the industry, to be La Salle's wine chemist. Previously, Otto had produced wines for Morris at the Windsor Wine Company after gaining experience in renowned wineries of Germany, his native country.

La Salle used Michigan grapes to produce port, Concord and muscatel. Blue Concord grape varieties were used to produce dark wines. Niagara grape varieties were used to produce white wines. Delaware grape varieties were used to produce sherry. Roughly 800,000 pounds of grapes were purchased each year from the vineyards of Paw Paw, Lawton and Milford. The wines were sweetened with Michigan-produced sugar. The winery also produced Sauternes, Riesling (Rhine), Tokay, Catawba, Champagne and sparkling Burgundy. Labeling wines with names and varietals was not regulated as it is today. Rather, these were seen as generic names reflecting a style of wine. La Salle's popular wine labels included Windsor Club, Royal Windsor and Cat and the Fiddle—"The wine that always keeps you in tune."

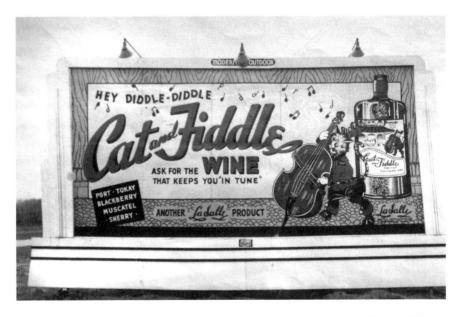

La Salle Wines and Champagne promotes Cat and the Fiddle wine brand. *Courtesy of St. Julian Wine Company.*

Upon the opening of the winery, the Michigan Liquor Control Commission (MLCC) placed a large order for La Salle wines to sell in the state's retail stores, the legal retailing process of wines at the time. This order set the winery's distribution in motion. La Salle wines were also on the wine lists of several Detroit-area restaurants, and its Champagne and Burgundy were distributed nationally. La Salle's wines were immediately in high demand.

In 1939, Morris built Michigan's first automated bottling room to manage his high production volume. He established warehouses in Flint, Grand Rapids, Battle Creek and Marquette to make distribution across the state even more efficient. By 1941, La Salle was producing almost half the wine in the state, topping more than 475,510 gallons, almost 200,000 cases, by 1966.

Three decades after Morris established the state's largest winery, he passed away in 1963. Wine production in Farmington continued until 1970, when the La Salle label was acquired by St. Julian Wine Company. St. Julian produced the wines for eight years using the original formulas before discontinuing them in 1978, ending the dynamic legacy of La Salle Wines and Champagne, Inc.

Today, the old La Salle winery is a registered historical site converted to an antique store and offices, some of which are located within the former wine vats. The winery can be toured each year during an annual haunted house event around Halloween.

St. Julian Wine Company

Soon after Prohibition was repealed in Michigan, Mariano Meconi relocated his wine business from Windsor to Detroit to take advantage of the recently opened market. The move to the United States proved prudent, as many Italian-Canadian men were detained in prison camps when Canada entered World War II. Meconi Wine Company became Michigan's fourth bonded winery and ultimately played a major role in the revitalization of Michigan's legal wine industry, which had disappeared with Prohibition.

One of Mariano's first endeavors was to produce wines for Kroger under a "Kroger" label he created for the grocery chain and sold only within the company's stores. To produce wines, Mariano traveled west for a couple of years from his Detroit wine facility to the well-established vineyards along the Lake Michigan shoreline to collect grapes. During a particularly challenging trek in wintry weather, he decided it was time to move his production closer to the grapes.

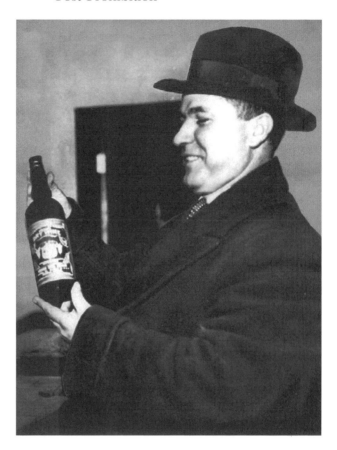

Mariano Meconi,
founder of St. Julian
Wine Company.
*Courtesy of St. Julian
Wine Company.*

In 1936, he relocated his winemaking operations to Paw Paw after purchasing the former Paw Paw Canning Company facility strategically located alongside the railroad. Ice blocks from Lake Michigan arrived by railroad and were used in the cellar to keep grapes cool to prevent early fermentation. In turn, these ice blocks were also used to preserve grapes during transport by railway to the Chicago market. The relocation prompted a name change to the Italian Wine Company to honor his heritage.

Mariano made varied wines, including Meconi Dry, increasing his product line and production volume at a conservative and steady pace over the decades. One of his biggest-selling products in the 1930s and 1940s was Sholom, a sweet Concord wine, under one of the winery's labels, St. Julian. The Kosher-certified Sholom is still produced by the winery today.

The St. Julian label, one of Mariano's early prevalent brands, paid homage to San Giuliano, the patron saint of his birthplace in Faleria, Italy. The wine

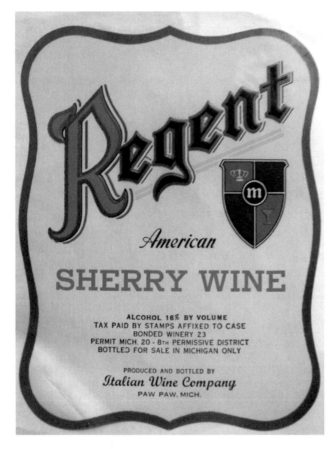

Left: A Regent wine label on sherry wine produced by the Italian Wine Company. *Courtesy of St. Julian Wine Company.*

Below: Big-seller of the era, Kosher-certified Sholom wine is still produced today. *Courtesy of St. Julian Wine Company.*

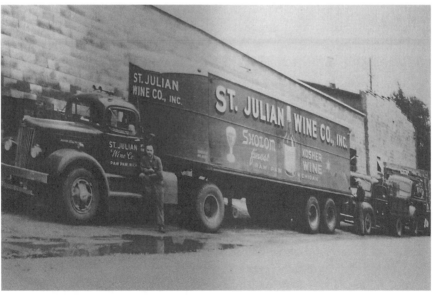

was quite popular, and production steadily increased. In 1940, Mariano installed an assembly line using an automated conveyor belt for labeling and sealing wines, giving the winery the capacity to produce 350,000 gallons of wine each year.

In 1941, Mariano was prompted to change his winery name once again. The bombing of Pearl Harbor on December 7 motivated him to change his company name within the week to St. Julian Wine Company to counter antifascist sentiment in the United States, though the name was not officially recognized by the State of Michigan until January 6, 1942.

Soon, Mariano began to grow his own Delaware, Concord and Niagara grapes to produce his wines. Over the ensuing years, he acquired several vineyards, eventually owning approximately eight hundred to nine hundred acres of farmland in Allegan, Van Buren and Berrien Counties.

In 1946, St. Julian produced sparkling wine for the first time after installing four Charmant tanks, each able to ferment up to one thousand gallons of wine at a time. Nine additional tanks have been added since then, and by 1991, St. Julian was processing sixteen thousand gallons of "effervescent wine." Within the next decade, though, St. Julian saw production drop to around five thousand cases due to price competition, and it refocused on other products.

Back in the 1950s, Interstate 94 was constructed alongside Paw Paw, beginning a new era for St. Julian. Mariano's son-in-law, Apollo (Paul) Braganini, vice-president, co-winemaker and plant manager at the time, began offering tours of the winemaking facility and opened a tasting room for the flood of tourists traveling the highway corridor. This also prompted the development of "nonalcoholic Champagne" to appease the youngest visitors, who tagged along with their parents into the tasting room. The company's still popular sparkling juice line was produced with grapes, cherries and apples grown in the region, and production exceeded 150,000 cases annually.

Also in the 1950s, St. Julian expanded with a distributorship in Detroit to increase the marketing of the company's wines. Mariano's son, Eugene, oversaw the sales force of twenty-five who sold imported and domestic wines, along with St. Julian's product line. Eugene's experience prepared him to serve as president of St. Julian, which became one of only two wineries to persevere as the industry faced challenges in the ensuing decades.

BRONTE CHAMPAGNE AND WINES COMPANY

Bronte Champagne and Wines Company was another of Michigan's most prolific wineries to open upon the repeal of Prohibition. The winery was established on May 26, 1933, six months before the national repeal, by Detroit real estate developer John Corsi. John, a father of ten children, immigrated to Ohio from Rome, Italy, in 1913, though John eventually made his way to Detroit. To start his winery, he sought additional business investors in Dr. Theodore Wozniak, Dr. Bernard Wozniak and Michael Rota. At the time, the Wozniaks, brothers with an additional eight siblings, were practicing dentists. The partners strategically went public with their company, selling 170,000 shares for only one dollar a share. This public, low cost approach enabled the businessmen to attract investors during the Great Depression.

Interestingly, one of Bronte's most notable shareholders was Charlie Gehringer, a renowned Detroit Tiger baseball star who played for the Tigers from 1924 to 1942 and was inducted in the National Baseball Hall of Fame in 1949. Robert Wozniak, son of founder Theodore and later the president of Bronte, shared that Charlie attended most stockholder meetings and often bought cases of Bronte wine.

The additional capital invested by stockholders was used to convert an old three-story Columbia Brewery building in downtown Detroit into a fully operating wine production facility. The construction included a semiautomatic bottling unit, rows of oak aging casks and glass-lined fermenting tanks to aid in the production of the wine. Upon completion, the brewery-turned-winery had the capacity to produce 800,000 gallons of wine each year.

From the start, the vintners aggressively produced and distributed Bronte wine, investing in a fleet of 1939 panel trucks and expanding their business to be a wholesaler of California and European wines. Bronte's twenty-five-man sales force kept busy distributing wines to five thousand accounts in Wayne, Oakland and Macomb Counties. Popular Bronte brands included Royal Bouquet, Italian Maid and Corsican.

In 1937, John recruited Angelo Spinazze to take charge of the winemaking operations. Angelo, who remained with the company for the next forty-seven years, was an Italian immigrant and graduate of the Italian viticultural school in Conegliano and was previously a winemaker for Major Maurice (Morris) R. Twomey in Windsor before he was hired by Bronte.

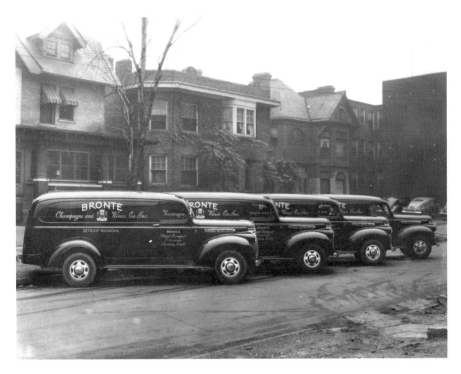

Bronte's fleet of 1939 panel trucks was used to distribute wines to five thousand accounts in Wayne, Oakland and Macomb Counties. *Courtesy of Robert Wozniak.*

In 1943, Bronte executives purchased a historic 150-acre farm in Hartford, located in southwest Michigan, to grow their own vineyards. Previously, grapes were purchased from growers and trucked to the Detroit facility from outlying farms. Notably, the new site was once home to the famous Keeler Donnybrook Harness Races from 1901 and 1913. Even before this, the Keeler branch of the Women's Christian Temperance Union was established in 1879 in the farmhouse on the property, a fact that the Bronte management team found incredibly ironic.

The farmhouse stood on one of the four corners in the main intersection of the village of Keeler. It was immediately remodeled and redecorated. A twenty-thousand-square-foot building was added to host the new winemaking facility. The new building was constructed with steel from an old foundry, as new steel was difficult to obtain during the war. Cypress wine storage tanks from Al Capone's Kankakee, Illinois brewery were situated in the main cellar of the winery. A total of forty-four cypress and oak aging tanks held fifteen thousand gallons of wine each, and seven glass-lined tanks held twenty thousand gallons each.

The first vines were added to the farm in the spring of 1943. Angelo oversaw the planting of the new grapevines by German prisoners of war who were imprisoned at the old county fairgrounds in nearby Hartford during World War II. By 1949, the vineyard had seventy thousand vines of Moore's Early, Niagara, Diamond, Ives and Norton varieties. Angelo worked mostly from Detroit, except during harvest. He spent the season in the vineyard to oversee the grape harvest. He worked closely with the winery's chemist, John Dohrow, to develop distinct wine styles. As a viticulturist and enologist, Angelo directed the vineyards and finessed the wines. John oversaw the washing of the grapes, crushing and fermentation before sending the wine to Detroit for further aging and bottling.

Also in 1949, John Corsi left the partnership with the Wozniaks due to business differences. John purchased Risdon Wines and Champagne in Detroit and transported the wine from the Bronte tanks to the tanks in his new facility.

In 1951, Angelo and his family, along with the winery offices and the entire production, moved to the vineyard in Hartford after the Detroit property was sold to developers. Angelo, who believed that the key of a good winemaker was quality blending, began to experiment with grape varietals and other fruits, eventually producing thirty-seven table wines and six sparkling wines from eleven different grape varieties. The winery produced Sauternes, Chablis, sherry, Burgundy, Delaware and Rhine, using renowned regional names, though the wines were typically used with grapes from the vineyard and supplemented, as needed, with grapes from California. Most wineries of this era used these names generically to express a style of wine.

In 1955, annual production exceeded 400,000 gallons. By the end of this era, Bronte's sales volume was high, and operations were effective. Angelo and John were working well together and began to pioneer notable products, releases that played a pivotal role in the upcoming era of the wine industry.

Risdon Wines and Champagne/ Frontenac Winery

When Mariano Meconi made his move to Paw Paw in 1936, he sold his Detroit wine production facility to C. Roland Risdon and Charles R. Risdon, owners of Risdon Wines and Champagne, founded in 1933. Before the sale, Mariano partnered with the Risdons in the production of wine.

The facility featured a semiautomated bottling unit, fermenting vats and oak aging casks and had the capacity to produce 250,000 gallons of wine each year. The winery quickly gained a national reputation for its Imperial Castle Champagne, aged in its natural-process Champagne-aging cellar. The Champagne was sold in Michigan, Chicago and other cities near the state border. The Risdons also acquired the Kroger label and continued producing wines for the grocery chain for several years.

Eventually, the Risdons realized that the wine business wasn't for them and sold Risdon Wines and Champagne to John Corsi in 1949, when John split from Bronte. John moved the business to Paw Paw and renamed it to Frontenac Winery. By 1962, the winery was producing 187,290 gallons of wine with the capacity to reach 500,000 gallons. Frontenac quickly became known for cocktail wines, and in 1964, two of John's products—Lemon Smash and Cherry Chantilly—won silver and gold medals at the Budapest International Wine Competition.

The Corsi family owned and operated the winery until 1967, when an investor group acquired it. Spirits broker E.J. Wieferman was president, and John Corsi's son, Carl Corsi, continued as a manager. The new investors immediately put $250,000 into expansion and modernization.

A new focus on dessert and cocktail wines included a colorful selection of forty-two flavors, such as Kafé D-Almond, a Kahlua-flavored wine; a spicy Candy Apple Red; and Schnappy Apple, a natural apple-flavored wine cocktail. The bestseller was Peach and Honey Smash, which was recommended to be served hot. New label designs had bright colors and sliced fruit.

E.J., a self-proclaimed Elvis junkie, released a wine two years after Elvis's death in 1977, called Always Elvis. The wine was crafted from grapes grown in Venice, Italy, and was limited to 100,000 cases. The wine gained national attention, both bad and good. Some people felt that it was wrong for the multitude of companies producing Elvis products to profit from his legacy, while others thought it was a nice tribute to his life (although a few thought that Elvis on a wine bottle was not a great way to capture his life since Elvis did not drink alcohol). Regardless, the Always Elvis wine bottles remain a desired collectible item today.

The fun attitude of the winery and products was expressed in a winery mural depicting young, charming monks in a wine lab, clearly enjoying their work. Today, the mural can be seen on the wall of the Lawton Community Center and Museum.

Frontenac wines were distributed to seven states. Most of the winery's consumers were senior citizens and younger consumers who were just learning about wine. To meet the demand of drier-style wines, the winery purchased vineyards in France, Spain, Italy and Germany and introduced five new red and white wines in 1982, produced from French-American hybrid varieties.

Interestingly, the winery changed its capping from corks to screw caps. Wine master Donald Bower may have been wise before his time when he decided that the screw top was better for the quality of the wine. The winery continued until its closing at some point in the late 1980s.

HOUPPERT WINE COMPANY

William C. Houppert was another vintner who opened a winery following Michigan's repeal of prohibition. William came from a long line of winemakers from the Alsace-Lorraine region of France and was passionate about winemaking, which he learned from his father, Franz. Franz, who planted a vineyard and opened a winery in Indianapolis upon immigrating to the United States, sold wines to consumers all over the nation for twenty-five years, until Prohibition closed his business.

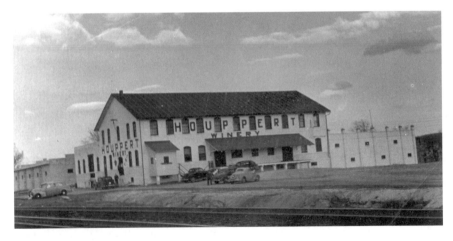

Houppert Wine Company opened in the former J.R. Day Grape Juice Company building in Lawton. *Courtesy of Rosemary Wade.*

Eventually, William moved to the Lawton region, which he had learned was a great fruit belt region and offered a profitable future for farmers who were willing to grow grapes for wine. From the start, he was interested in producing table wines like those produced in Europe.

To open his budding business, William secured a mortgage with John Turner of the First National Bank of Lawton for $55,000 in 1933 to purchase the former J.R. Day Grape Juice Company building in Lawton. William hired Robert Wade, a childhood friend of his late son's, as a chemist and winemaking apprentice. The wines produced by the duo quickly earned a stellar reputation, and the winery prospered, operating seven days a week.

In 1937, William expanded his business by selling raw cream of tartar, generated from the lees of wine. This deep red raw tartar was created by pressing and baking the juice from the lees. He marketed 120 barrels of the tartar to baking powder companies that bought, refined and bleached the raw product.

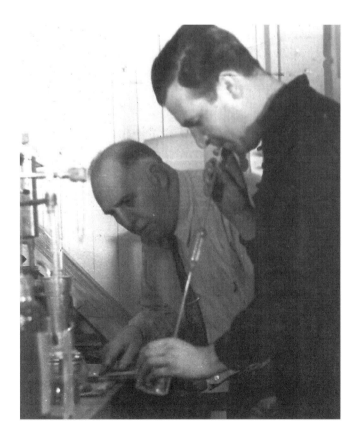

William Houppert and Robert Wade in the Houppert Wine Company laboratory. *Courtesy of Rosemary Wade.*

In 1939, an abundant crop caused him to ramp up the capacity of his winery from 300,000 to 500,000 gallons. He added new tanks and a fermenting cellar. At the same time, Robert experimented with strawberry, cherry and rhubarb wines.

Disaster struck, though, when a spark from a passing steam locomotive allegedly landed on the roof of the building, igniting a catastrophic fire on June 7, 1940. The building's brick and frame walls remained standing after the blaze, though the inside of the building was gutted.

Imported French wine casks dating from seventy-five to more than one hundred years old were destroyed, and around 100,000 gallons of wine were lost in the fire. The wine was released from the main storage vats to prevent explosions and possible danger to life. It poured out of the building, forming a lake that was scooped up by scavengers.

Determined to rebuild his beloved winery, William returned to the business the same year after reconstructing the building using massive cobblestones hauled in from area farms. Unfortunately, he was unable to rebuild the business aspect of the winery. In 1943, the Houppert Wine Company collapsed.

MICHIGAN WINERIES/WARNER VINEYARDS

In the meantime, John Turner purchased the Puritan Wine Company in nearby Paw Paw. The winery, originally the Puritan Grape Juice Company, had converted its grape juice production to winemaking in 1933, just days after the state legalization of commercial alcohol production. John had been growing grapes with his brother since 1904, so becoming a vintner wasn't an all-encompassing new venture for him.

John spent $100,000 to modernize the production facility, preparing it for his new winery, which was named Michigan Wineries. He partnered with Andrew Murch to run the overall operations of the business. John was more of a silent business partner, concerned foremost with the financials of the company.

Andrew's son, John Murch, recalled, "We'd visit John Turner on the weekends, so my dad could give him updates on the business, and John could give input on the financials."

Besides producing wines at the new facility, Michigan Wineries also received, processed and crushed grapes for Milan Wine Company of Detroit.

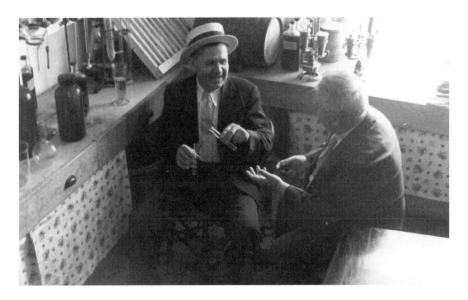

John Turner of Michigan Wineries meets with a Houppert Wine Company customer. *Courtesy of Rosemary Wade.*

After the demise of nearby Houppert Wine Company, Andrew and John acquired the winery and equipment and hired Robert Wade, Houppert's chemist, as chief winemaker. These transactions further solidified Michigan Wineries' place in the winemaking business.

The Rosalie and Ambassador Club wine labels carried over from Houppert Wine Company to Michigan Wineries. A photograph of a woman was featured on the original Rosalie bottle, although over the years the label changed to a drawing. Fortified dessert wines, including muscatel, dark and light port and several styles of sherry, were produced and sold under these labels for a couple of decades.

In the 1940s, an abundance of grapes was still available from the vineyards growing in the region. The financially astute John Turner saw an opportunity and established the Paw Paw Juice Company in 1944, diversifying his products.

Unfortunately, the partnership of Michigan Wineries only lasted a few years due to business differences, and in 1949, John bought Andrew's stock. Andrew started A.F. Murch Company to produce and sell Champagne for mail order, a booming business in New York at the time. Sometime after 1962, the sparkling wine business didn't work out for Andrew, so he ventured into the grape and apple juice concentrate business. He eventually sold his

Paw Paw business to Smucker's, which, in turn, sold to Coca-Cola. The Coca-Cola plant still exists today.

In the 1950s, John established the Cask brand to compete with California wine giant E.J. Gallo Winery. Originally labeled Cask 59, it is believed that the 59 represented the first year of the brand, though the 59 was dropped from the label at some point over the years. The new label included table and dessert wines made with Niagara, Concord and some Delaware grapes. At one time, more than thirty wines were marketed under the Cask brand, which was produced into the 1990s. By 1951, John's son-in-law, James K. Warner, had taken over as president, running a wine business that was gearing up for major expansion to become the state's next largest winery.

PAW PAW WINE COMPANY

Shortly after the repeal of national Prohibition, Antoni (Tony) Misuraca established the American Wine Company in Detroit in 1934. His experience in winemaking was learned as a child apprentice in his native land of Sicily, which he left at age fourteen to live with his uncle in Detroit. After operating his winery for six years, Tony followed the lead of many of the other Detroit vintners and moved his operations to Paw Paw. In 1940, he took over the V. and J. Winery, which only lasted a few years after its establishment in 1937.

The following year, he began the production of six thousand to seven thousand gallons of wine under the label, Virginia Wines, as contracted by the General Beverage Company of Detroit, makers of Virginia Dare soft drinks. The wines were distributed by twenty-two representatives across the country.

Tony renamed his business to the Paw Paw Wine Company and produced wines under four different labels: Misuraca Wines, Gloria Wines, Paw Paw Wines and Tony Fine Wines. Most of his wines were produced from Niagara, Concord and Delaware grapes, though Tony quickly gained a reputation as an experimental winemaker by crafting small batches of creative wines from cherry, apple, dandelion and tomato. In fact, it is believed that Tony produced the first commercial rhubarb wine in America, of which he developed two types: white from green fruit and pink from the ripe rhubarb. The wine was unfortified but sweetened with sugar.

Unfortunately, Tony's winemaking career ended in 1961, when the Paw Paw Wine Company dissolved. Restless in retirement, Tony and his wife started a successful spaghetti sauce line, called Mama Misuraca's Italian Spaghetti Sauce, that continued for years.

Molly Pitcher Wines: A Winery with Many Names

In early 1934, Irishman William Ruttledge established Chateau Wines Corporation in Royal Oak. William, who emigrated from County Galway, Ireland, in 1908, was influenced by his uncle, who produced wine and tea in Dublin. Upon the repeal of national Prohibition, he convinced William, a graduate in engineering, to drop his pump manufacturing business in Detroit and start a winery to take advantage of the newly opened opportunity.

William immediately started production of only port, the favorite wine in Ireland at the time, until he realized that Michigan consumers did not have similar tastes as his native Irishmen. Fortunately, he was quick to note this difference and diversified. He experienced expedient growth and produced wines in his Detroit facility, which had the bottling capacity of eight thousand bottles a day and the production capacity of 205,000 gallons a year.

In 1947, William relocated his winery near the shore of Lake Michigan in Harbert and renamed it the Molly Pitcher Winery for heroine Mary Hays McCauley. Mary gained notoriety after taking over her husband's cannon when he was wounded in battle. Molly Pitcher was a nickname given to women of the American Revolution who carried water to soldiers during combat.

The winery immediately garnered a reputation for its wines. At its peak, Molly Pitcher was capable of producing one thousand cases of wines in a day and was the largest grape processor in Berrien County, with sales branches in Muskegon, Marquette, Grand Rapids, Kalamazoo, Detroit and Lansing.

In December 1953, the winery celebrated its upcoming twenty-year anniversary. At this time, William's son, Eamon, who was vice-president and general manager at the time, assisted in overseeing the winery's three additional branches in Marquette, Royal Oak and Moline.

As production continued to rise, a brand-new facility was constructed in 1957 to host the winery's offices and laboratory. Unfortunately, thieves set fire to the facility in 1974, causing extensive damage to offices and the laboratory, though no wine was damaged. That same year, at age ninety, William was ready to retire and sold the winery. His son, Eamon, who was sixty-five years old, retired along with his father. At the time of the sale, the winery was producing 500,000 gallons of wine and had four acres of vineyards.

Cecil E. and Betty Pond became the new owners of the winery and renamed it to the Lakeside Vineyard Company, making drier-style wines under the Lakeside label while retaining the Molly Pitcher brand for the winery's sweet line of wines. The Ponds operated Lakeside Vineyard for the next nine years. Leonard Olson, who had co-founded Tabor Hill Winery of Buchanan in 1970, assumed ownership of the Lakeside Vineyard Company in 1983. He renamed the winery to Olson Family Wine Cellars. Unfortunately, Len experienced several health issues and was unable to continue operation of his new winery, which only lasted two years.

Don Kennedy acquired the winery and renamed it to Berrien Vintner Cellars. Don retained ownership until his untimely death in 1991, at which time the winery was disbanded.

Today, the building is home to high-end condominiums. Several of the concrete vats are integrated into individual home designs.

MILAN WINERIES COMPANY

Milan Wineries was established more than a decade after the other wineries. Charles Milan, Florence Milan and Robert Rubinstein established a winery in 1944 in Detroit, which became one of Michigan's largest producers for a brief period.

High-selling labels included Milan's Cadillac Club, Cadillac Club Reserve, Cadillac Club DeLuxe and Nature Boy. Another label was called Lakeshore Reserve. Milan Wineries earned a reputation for its "pop wines," which were sweet and inexpensive and very popular with the "winos." A semiautomatic bottling unit kept production moving along at a timely pace, and in 1962, Milan was the state's biggest producer, with a production level that reached 681,138 gallons. Unfortunately, the winery closed sometime after 1975.

LAPEER WINERY

Romanian immigrant Joseph Wakaresku arrived in Lapeer in 1905 and, three decades later, in 1935, established the Lapeer Winery, the only Lake Huron winery in the immediate post-Prohibition era. Joseph was an experienced winemaker who derived from several generations of winemakers from the small town of Beba, Romania. He established his winery by producing wines from a forty-five-acre vineyard he leased from Horace H. Davis, who had previously planted two thousand grapevines each year for several years on his two-hundred-acre farm. Joseph produced three wine labels named Golden Harvest, Lucky Star and Empress of Michigan and twelve varieties, including Rhine, Sauternes, Burgundy, Claret, Chianti, Port, Tokay, White Port, Sherry, Muscatel, Elderberry and Apple.

By 1937, he was producing fifty thousand gallons of wine annually. The wines were distributed throughout the state, across the nation and into Canada. The following year, the Lapeer Winery burned down. Joseph opened a new winery three years later in a new location, designing his tasting room as an Old English alehouse. The winery closed six years later in 1947.

MICHIGAN WINE INSTITUTE

A key contributor toward the success of the Michigan wine industry in the decades following post-Prohibition was the cohesiveness of the state's wine producers. In 1938, the state's first wine lobbying and promotional organization, the Michigan Wine Institute, was established by the state's eight existing wineries. Founding members included La Salle Wines and Champagne Company, Italian Wine Company, Bronte Champagnes and Wine Company, Houppert Wine Company, Michigan Wineries, Chateau Wines Corporation, Risdon Wines and Champagne and Lapeer Winery.

Mariano Meconi, the institute's first president, led the wineries to focus on promoting native Michigan wines, lobbying for legal issues affecting their industry and strengthening relationships with growers. The institute encouraged the planting of grape varietals that were most desirable for producing wine at the time—Niagara and Delaware—and agreed to purchase surpluses of the farmers' other fruits, including apples and peaches. The members of the institute also paid growers top prices for their grapes. Growth in wine production was spurred by the strong partnership between the state's wineries and wine grape growers. Michigan quickly became a leader in the industry, behind California and New York, and production continued to rise over the next couple of decades.

HOW SWEET IT IS

Michigan's wineries created a well-established industry quickly after the repeal of Prohibition. At the very beginning, the industry struggled to sell its products, as consumers preferred wines crafted from other states using grape varietals other than the "foxy"-tasting Concord. However, in 1937, Maurice (Morris) Twomey proposed a law placing a tax of fifty cents per gallon on out-of-state wines and only four cents per gallon on Michigan wines, providing that they had been produced with at least 75 percent Michigan grapes and that the vintner had paid at least fifty-five dollars per ton for the grapes. The law was written by William C. Geagley, chief chemist of the Michigan Department of Agriculture.

The new law, albeit somewhat odd, protected the state from out-of-state wine competition, and demand for Michigan wines by Michigan consumers increased dramatically. In 1939 and 1940, the state produced over 1,000,000 gallons, almost 500,000 cases, of wine. By 1942, production had reached 1,250,000 gallons, and this was maintained through the remainder of the 1940s. Naturally, the majority of the wine was sold within the state. Incidentally, in 1972, the law was modified, increasing the amount required to pay for grapes for a second time from $85 to $100 a ton, causing a handful of wineries to shut down operations.

Another law written and influenced by William stated that all wine consisting of more than 16 percent alcohol content would be categorized as hard liquor. Since the production of liquor required a $5,000 licensing fee and alternative distribution, Michigan vintners were financially limited to producing fortified wines that were 16 percent alcohol or less. At the same time, federal law considered fortified wines to be a minimum of 16 percent alcohol. Therefore, the fortified wines Michigan was producing required "lightly fortified" on the label.

As sugar was rationed during World War II, there was a huge pent-up demand for sweet wine when the war ended in 1945. To satisfy the sweet palates of Americans and their preference for sweet wines, winemakers fortified the natural juices with the addition of sugar and already-fortified wine or brandy. The more fortified the wine, the sweeter it is. These fortified wines were the preferred drink of choice.

Since Michigan wine was lower in alcohol content than wines produced elsewhere, the state's wines were less desirable to the consumer. California started controlling the market with wines fortified closer to 20 percent alcohol content. The stability of the Michigan wine industry was once again in jeopardy.

In 1950, a law passed enabling Michigan wineries to produce wines closer to 20 percent alcohol, which meant that the wines could now be considered fortified rather than distilled spirits. It also allowed the higher-fortified wines to be distributed and sold along with other wines in grocery stores. In addition, it eliminated the $5,000 licensing fee. This change boosted the state's wine industry by improving the competition against California. Michigan wineries flourished by producing wines using Niagara, Concord and Delaware grapes. The demand for muscatels, ports, sherries and other fruit wines exploded. Michigan's sweet wine production took a dramatic leap, and by the early 1960s, the state's industry was at its peak, producing 2,299,500 gallons, almost 1,000,000 cases, each year.

VISIONARIES AND SURVIVALISTS

The 1960s and 1970s

Americans loved their wines, and a notable increase in wine consumption was now evident. Through the 1960s, this consumption rose roughly 60 percent in the United States. In the early part of this era, Michigan retained its stronghold in the marketplace and was the third largest producer of wine in the nation, behind California and New York. Remarkably, the early 1960s were the pinnacle of Michigan's wine production to date.

With this new era came a noticeable change in the styles of preferred wines. The American palate had evolved from preferring sweet and fortified wines to favoring drier-style wines. Consumers were demanding table wines that were more pleasing to savor and more complementary to meals. This change in the market was largely influenced by a few key factors. First, American soldiers, formerly stationed in Europe, had a new appreciation for palatable table wines. Furthermore, the influence of new celebrities, like cookbook author and television personality Julia Child, was educating Americans on how to cook and pair foods with wine. Overall, American wine drinkers were becoming savvier and more knowledgeable about wines, and table wines were the new vogue. In 1969, the consumption of table wines surpassed the consumption of sweet wines for the first time in the nation's history.

Michigan vintners were aware of this evolution and began plotting how to evolve their wines for the marketplace. As early as 1957, the state's nine wineries started a commission of experts from each of the wineries to meet twice a month, conduct blind tastings of their wines and evaluate the quality. Their objective was to improve the overall quality of Michigan wines and steer consumers away from out-of-state brands.

Within a few years, different styles of wine had spurred new vineyard plantings in northern and southern Michigan. However, most of Michigan's vintners, while moving in the right direction, were slow to implement the necessary changes.

California vintners, on the other hand, were much quicker to react. Innovations enabled them to mass produce affordable and improved table wines and distribute wines across the country to meet the demand. California giant E.J. Gallo Winery executed tactics to maintain the winery's prevalent share of the Michigan market.

To make matters worse, a detrimental state law change in 1972 literally shut down operations for some of Michigan's biggest wineries. By 1973, wine production had significantly dropped to only 600,000 cases, almost all of which were sweet wines. Michigan's instate market share, which was once 80 percent, dropped to less than 30 percent by 1975. Production continued to drop through the rest of the 1970s, though the Michigan wineries that survived were implementing the necessary changes to meet the evolving style of preferred wines.

For the most part, Michigan's first French-American hybrid and European vinifera varietals for commercial winemaking were planted in the 1960s and 1970s, although Bronte Champagne and Wine Company unveiled Michigan's first serious table wine as early as 1962. Michigan Wineries (now Warner Vineyards) began planting French-American hybrids in the late 1960s after extensive research in New York and Ontario. St. Julian followed suit with new hybrid plantings in the early 1970s. New vintners entering the market from the mid-1960s to the early 1970s focused on producing table wines from the advent of their wineries. A new journey for Michigan vintners had begun.

Bronte Champagne and Wines Company Makes State's First Notable Table Wine

Angelo Spinazze was a spirited winemaker who was passionate about making styles of wine reflective of the Old World. His Italian upbringing and education heavily influenced his winemaking from the start of his North American career. In 1954, with support from Bronte executives, Angelo

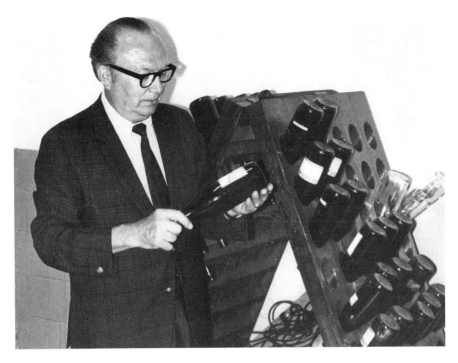

Angelo Spinazze among bottles of Bronte wine. *Courtesy of Robert Wozniak.*

planted Baco Noir, a French-American hybrid grape, and produced the state's first commercial wine from a French-American hybrid. As a side note, John Leban, a grower in Sodus Township near the Bronte vineyards, planted what is believed to be the first Baco Noir in Michigan in the 1930s.

Bronte's Baco Noir earned praise from renowned wine writer Leon Adams, who called it outstanding. It was also selected as the top wine by Bob Damoth of the American Wine Society at a *Detroit News* wine tasting of nine red table wines from around the world.

Along with the first plantings of Baco Noir, Bronte was also first to plant Seibel 5279, a white French-American hybrid grape now known as Aurora. With these plantings, Angelo proved that Michigan could succeed in growing and producing French-American hybrid varietals in the cold-climate conditions.

During a newspaper interview, Angelo stated:

> *We are blessed with a climate comparable to the wine growing areas of France. We have the winds off Lake Michigan to delay budding in the*

spring until danger of frost is over and the same winds keep the danger of frost low in the fall to allow the grapes to mature. When we first began experimenting with the French hybrids years ago, people said we couldn't grow them here. They said it just couldn't be done. Well, we proved them wrong.

First to Bottle Cold Duck in the United States

Another feat by Bronte was the release of Cold Duck, the nation's first bottling of this popular wine. Cold Duck originated in the Bavarian region of Germany, where cold, sparkling Burgundy was mixed with previously opened Champagne. This combination was nicknamed *kalte ende* (cold end), which, in America, was quickly altered to *kalte ente* (cold duck).

Pontchartrain Wine Cellars in Detroit was a pioneer of Cold Duck in the United States. Owner Harold Borgman combined still Burgundy wine with sparkling wine starting in 1937.

In the early 1960s, Robert Wozniak, now president of Bronte Champagne and Wines Company, and some of his colleagues visited Pontchartrain Wine Cellars and enjoyed the taste of Borgman's Cold Duck. Robert immediately encouraged Angelo to develop the wine. Angelo blended Baco Noir, Delaware and some other grapes before fermenting them together and applying the Charmat, or bulk, method for sparkling wine. Initially, Robert had some difficulties gaining wine label approval from the Alcohol and Tobacco Tax and Trade Bureau (TTB), as the agency had never heard of the wine style before.

Upon its release into the marketplace in 1964, Bronte's Cold Duck became the winery's bestselling wine as it flew off the shelves. Robert proudly recalled placing fifty cases of Cold Duck on end caps in a store on Friday and, by Monday, having to replace the stock.

One vintner who immediately took notice of Bronte's success with Cold Duck was Ernest Gallo. Ernest called Robert in the 1960s, inquiring about Bronte's wine that was rapidly selling in the marketplace. By 1971, Gallo's own Cold Duck–styled wine, André, had become a well-known national brand.

In the meantime, Robert had success getting Bronte Champagne and Cold Duck on wine menus at the Grand Hotel on Mackinac Island and in popular restaurants of Detroit. One in particular was Joe Muer's Restaurant, which closed in 1997 after sixty-nine years of serving Great Lakes and ocean

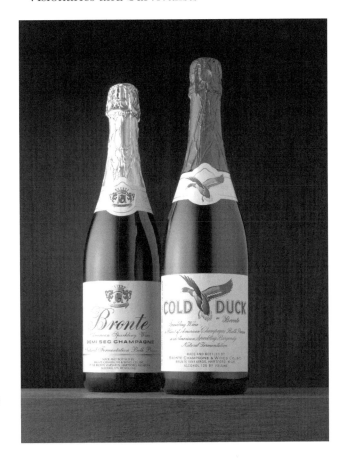

Bronte Champagne and Cold Duck, popular wines of the 1960s and 1970s. *Photograph by Howard Bjornson.*

seafood to the rich and powerful of the region. Bronte's bubblies were also featured at Sinbad's on the Detroit River, a former Prohibition-era speakeasy, and at Machus Red Fox, where Jimmy Hoffa was last sighted. Many more restaurants featured the wildly popular wines, including Zehnders in Frankenmuth and Schuler's Restaurant in Marshall.

"A tremendous amount of Cold Duck and Bronte Champagne were sold in split bottles, which were six ounce bottles of Champagne," said Robert. "These splits were very popular during this era."

Bronte continued to grow its fan base with its sparkling wines through the 1970s. Henry Ford II, grandson to Henry Ford, founder of the Ford Motor Company, and Anthony David "Champagne Tony" Lema were fans of Bronte Champagne, believed to have been first produced in the 1940s.

Anthony won back-to-back Buick Open Invitationals in Michigan in 1964 and 1965. His gregarious image was earned when he asked for Champagne after every win. In Michigan, he requested Bronte Champagne for his celebrations. Anthony's reputation as one of the world's greatest golfers of the era lives on, though sadly, he and his wife died when their plane crashed on a golf course in 1966. He was only thirty-two.

The same year that Cold Duck was released, Bronte began to offer free winery and vineyard tours. The twenty-five-minute tour took visitors through the wine cellars and along the bottling lines, where tour guides presented the production of wines, sherries and Champagnes. At the end of the tour, free wine sampling was available in the hospitality room. In 1972, these tours were at their peak, attracting seventy thousand visitors annually to the winery.

This was the same year that Angelo and his right-hand man, Curtis Frick, who succeeded John Dohrow in the 1960s, released four new wines, including Hartford cream sherry, a mellow, sweet sherry *cuvée*. The sherry was baked at 100 to 120 degrees for three months to get its nutty flavor. After baking, the sherry was transferred to small oak barrels for aging. Along with the popular Hartford cream sherry, four other sherries were produced at the winery.

"Our real achievements were in developing the Champagne business, planting French-American hybrid grapes and the production of premium dessert wines, like the Hartford cream sherry," said Robert.

Altogether, the winemaking team produced thirty still wines and six sparkling wines. By 1975, Bronte had distributed nearly 250,000 cases of wine and sparkling wine in the Midwest using thirty-four distributors. Within the next decade, though, the market changed significantly and had a devastating impact on Bronte's production levels, literally dropping them in half. In 1984, the management decided to cease operating one of Michigan's largest wineries of the era.

NORTHERN MICHIGAN'S FIRST MODERN-DAY VINEYARD: BOSKYDEL VINEYARD

Bernie Rink grew up amid vineyards in Ohio along Lake Erie in the 1930s, just south of where many of Michigan's post-Prohibition wineries were established. Fast-forward to the 1960s. Bernie was working as the library director at Northwestern Michigan College in Traverse City. A borrowed library book reignited Bernie's interest in vineyards and prompted him to plant northern Michigan's first modern-day vineyard in 1964.

He planted ten vines each of more than thirty varietals on a test basis on his Lake Leelanau property, situated on Leelanau Peninsula. His plantings included cold-hardy French-American hybrid grapes, as well as three varieties of European vinifera: Pinot Noir, Riesling and Chardonnay.

Bernie continued his role as librarian as his vineyard matured. Over seven years, he evaluated the varietals to determine which ones grew best in the region's often-fickle climate. A practical man, he selected the varietals he believed were hardy enough to withstand the cold climate, were not susceptible to disease, ripened early and made the best wine. In 1971, he planted fifteen acres of Soleil Blanc, Vignoles (formerly Ravat 51), Seyval, Aurore, De Chaunac and Cascade Noir. He also grew small numbers of other varieties, such as Marechal Foch, Baco Noir and Chancellor for blending. He stuck with French-American hybrids, believing in the dying vine theory of "the harder the vine has to struggle, the better the wine."

Throughout this period, Bernie collaborated with Dr. G. Stanley Howell of Michigan State University, inviting Howell and his students to research the varietals he was growing, some of which were unique to the state.

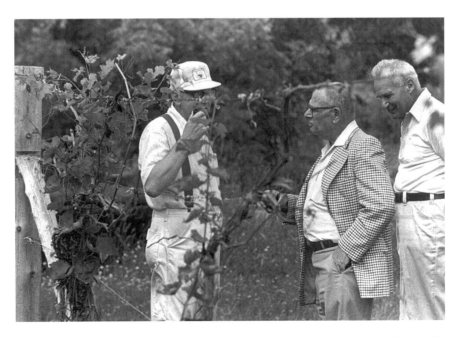

Bernie Rink, Leon Adams and Bob Herbst in Bernie's Lake Leelanau vineyard. *Courtesy of Boskydel Vineyard.*

On August 19, 1976, Bernie opened his tasting room, which he called Boskydel Vineyard, Leelanau Peninsula's first bonded winery. He produced 639 cases of wine his first year. The winery was named for the unpublished manuscript by Al Bungart called the "Elves of Bosky Dingle," a series of stories favored by his boys. Bernie also took pleasure in discovering that the word "bosky" means "befuddled, with drink, inebriated."

By the early 1980s, Boskydel had earned raves for his wines and no-nonsense style. Renowned wine writer Leon Adams referred to Bernie's wines as impressive in his 1985 version of *The Wines of America*. John J. Baxevanis, also a renowned wine writer, stated in *The Wine Regions of America* that Bernie's De Chaunac "may very well be the finest French-American wine in America." French sommelier Gerard Angelovici declared, "Boskydel Vineyard 1994 De Chaunac to be of exceptional quality and value."

Today, Bernie, at age eighty-three, continues to produce and serve the same wines he did in 1976, including five whites and four reds, all of which are 100 percent estate-grown and bottled. His dry humor and simple tasting room, haphazardly displaying favorite sayings and old newspaper articles, are an integral part of the northern Michigan wine experience.

FIRST BONDED WINERY SINCE POST-PROHIBITION BOOM: TABOR HILL WINERY

In 1968, businessman Carl Banholzer bought a farm on Mount Tabor Hill in Buchanan and partnered with steel salesman Leonard Olson to open a winery. Excited at the prospect of becoming full-time vintners, the two began researching varietals to plant in southwest Michigan's fruit belt.

They planted French-American hybrid varietals—Vidal Blanc and Aurora—the first year. A year later, they expanded the vineyard to include twenty-seven grape varietals, including Baco Noir, Marechal Foch, De Chaunac, Chamborcin, Cascade, Seyval, Vignoles and Michigan's first planting of vinifera varietals, Chardonnay and Riesling.

Notably, in 1970, Tabor Hill was the first new bonded winery since the plethora of wineries that opened after Prohibition was repealed in 1933. To house their winery and tasting room, Carl and Len contracted the construction of a chateau-style building. Today, the hilltop structure, with enhancements and expansion, is still the focal point of the vineyard.

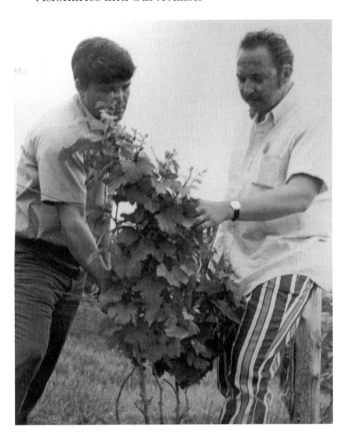

Leonard Olson and Carl Banholzer plant grapevines in the late 1960s. *Courtesy of Leonard Olson.*

The winemakers produced 673 cases the first year with two tons of Delaware grapes from a local vineyard and two and a half tons of young, tender plantings of their own Vidal Banc and Aurora grapes. Grapes were placed in sawed-in-half wine barrels and stomped after they found that crushing grapes by foot was much easier than hand-cranking the small grape presser.

Before long, philosophical business differences divided the partners before the 1971 harvest. Len took over the management and proceeded with the vision to add a ten-foot-deep underground cellar to store bottles, barrels and tanks of wine. By 1973, the winery was producing almost six thousand cases of wine. Len focused on winemaking, while Tim Cote managed the vineyard for the next ten years.

Tabor Hill immediately garnered national attention for the quality of wines. In 1974, President Gerald Ford hosted the ambassador from Austria at a White House state dinner and served Tabor Hill's 1971 Vidal Blanc. For at least five consecutive years thereafter, Tabor Hill wine was served at the White House.

Tabor Hill won six awards at the American Wine Competition in Washington, D.C., in 1977, including two silver medals for Rieslings and a bronze for Baco Noir.

By the mid-1970s, though, Len was struggling financially to maintain his budding business and began seeking investors to keep his winery in production. In 1979, Whirlpool heir David Upton bought the winery for $40,000 under a bulk sales act, though he used bank notes and income from his abstract and title business to purchase the winery.

NEW VINTNERS SELECT MICHIGAN TO ESTABLISH WINERY, FENN VALLEY VINEYARDS

North of Tabor Hill Winery, Chicago businessman William Welsch fulfilled his dream to become a farmer. In 1973, he and his son, Doug Welsch, embarked on a journey to learn about winemaking and began researching renowned wine regions, such as the Finger Lakes region of New York. The Welsches selected Michigan as the region to plant their vineyard. After visiting several potential sites along the west coast of the state, they acquired 230 acres of rolling landscape in Fennville within four miles of Lake Michigan's breezes.

The farm is nestled about midway on Michigan's west coast in the Lower Peninsula. It benefits from the westerly winds of Lake Michigan that temper the regional climate for ideal grape-growing conditions. Fruits grow well in the region. Within thirty miles of Fennville are orchards full of cherry, pear and plum trees and blueberry bushes.

The father-son team built a hillside winery to benefit from the natural cooling in the aging cellars. They initially planted French-American hybrids—Marechal Foch and Seyval—in 1974. The following year, they planted the first of several plantings of Riesling. For three more decades, they expanded their vineyard to include sixteen varietals on sixty-two acres.

In 1976, the Welsches held the grand opening of Fenn Valley Vineyards and produced twenty-one hundred cases of wine the first year. From the start, a self-guided tour, modeled after a similar tour by Sterling Vineyards in California, invited guests to overlook the winery from a balcony. In the 1980s, the Welsches began hosting summer gatherings of area Taster Guild members and dignitaries. Doug borrowed a farm tour wagon from the nearby MSU research farm to cart guests through the vineyards. By the late 1980s, they had constructed their own wagon, though it wasn't until the late 1990s that vineyard tours would take off.

A group representing the Saugatuck Bed-and-Breakfasts approached Doug about hosting weekend tours to encourage visits to the region during the autumn months. After several weeks with only a few customers in a wagon that could hold twenty people, they decided to open the tours to the public. Initially, interest was marginal; however, within two years, participation skyrocketed. This prompted Doug to contact the Michigan Liquor Control Commission to secure permission for wine tastings in the vineyard. In 1999, wine-tasting tours on the 160 acres of vineyards at Fenn Valley Vineyards were approved, an act that, Doug said, "makes ours the largest licensed tasting room in Michigan, if not the United States."

Today, three wagons are available to take guests of Fenn Valley into the vineyards. The tours include tastings of wine and ripe wine grapes from the vines.

Cellar tours were also launched in the mid-1990s, when Doug coordinated with area bed-and-breakfasts to promote Wine Lover's Weekend during the winter months. "The tours involve tasting from barrels and tanks, and often involve opening one or more older bottles of wine from our wine library," said Doug. "Little did I realize that I was planting the seeds for what would later be a driving force for our retail sales during the winter months."

Starting in 2005, guided cellar tours took off; today, they are so popular that reservations are required.

"The tour-and-tasting centers compare two or more examples of wines made from the same grapes where a winemaking process is changed. We are attempting to illustrate how practices in the cellar can affect a wine's style," explained Doug, who credited the tours as the driving force for their retail business, especially during the winter months of January and February.

By 2009, the winery was producing forty thousand cases of wine, and production is steadily increasing. More than sixty thousand people visit the tasting room each year, and nearly twenty-five hundred people sign up for the guided tours through the vineyard and winemaking facility. One thousand of these visitors take the tour in September and October alone.

FIRST 100 PERCENT EUROPEAN VINIFERA VINEYARD: CHATEAU GRAND TRAVERSE

Successful business executive Edward O'Keefe was a risk taker. A track record of owning several businesses in the Detroit area signified this feisty Irishman's passion for challenges and problem solving. Ed decided he wanted to make fine, European-style wines in northern Michigan. This was a bold move, considering vinifera grapes had not been proven to survive Michigan's volatile weather from year to year. This fact didn't deter him, though, as he felt his property on Old Mission Peninsula in Traverse City, strategically located on the same forty-fifth parallel as renowned grape-growing regions in Europe, was ideal for producing high-quality wines reflective of the Old World class of wines.

Before shifting substantial, self-raised dollars into a new vineyard, Ed first consulted with multiple German experts. Karl Werner, a seventeenth-generation winemaker, advised Ed to consult with Dr. Helmut Becker, who was a teacher (and later dean) of the renowned Geisenheim Oenological and Viticultural Institute.

Ed was quite determined to learn everything he could about world-class wines and funded a research trip to Europe, taking Dr. G. Stanley Howell of MSU and Len Olson of Tabor Hill Winery along with him. The trio visited Geisenheim to meet with Helmut. They also traveled to wineries in Italy, Switzerland, France and throughout Germany to increase their knowledge of growing vinifera vines to make European-style wines.

Ed persuaded Helmut to travel to Old Mission Peninsula and evaluate his site for a potential vineyard. Helmut advised him to reshape his fifty-five acres of land to gain the most benefit from his location situated between West and East Bay of Lake Michigan. Ed took Helmut's advice and prepared his land accordingly for the planting of vines.

In 1975, German viticulturalist Bernd Philippi, another expert introduced to Ed by Karl, oversaw the planting of the vineyard. Thirty acres of Riesling, Chardonnay and Merlot were planted on his beautiful fifty-five-acre rolling hillside. The vineyard was planted in the classic style of the Rhine region of Germany, which used closer vine spacing to allow the planting of about 1,066 vines per acre rather than the 750 found in most U.S. vineyards. A seven-wire parallel trellising system was implemented to make the vines grow vertical, allowing more exposure to sunlight. This produced more uniform ripening of bunches at the end of the growing season and facilitated more efficient vine care and harvesting. The new elevation of the land allowed for good air drainage—a way for cold air to flow down and out of the vineyard to avoid severe frost.

As a side note, Ed's decision to plant Merlot was quite amusing. Before planting his vines, Ed visited Bernie Rink's vineyards on nearby Leelanau Peninsula and saw flourishing grapevines. He asked Bernie about the varietal and misunderstood it for Merlot when Bernie told him it was Leon Millet. Ed immediately decided to plant several acres of the varietal, an accidental move that eventually proved prudent. Ed saw his decision of planting a 100 percent vinifera vineyard as a wise long-term investment, though many believed his decision was risky.

While waiting for the first harvest, Ed constructed a modern winemaking facility with mostly German-made equipment. Under Karl's direction, he modeled the winery after a winery in California. Incidentally, $38,000 was spent on integrating re-rods into the floor, following earthquake guidelines in California. Although this was unnecessary in Michigan, this accidental investment later proved sensible as the winery grew and its production expanded. The reinforced floor accommodated the extremely heavy production loads that would otherwise have required additional reinforcement.

In 1976, he established Chateau Grand Traverse, and by the end of the era, Ed had flourishing vineyards, a new winery and tasting room and two young sons being groomed to join the business. The winery was positioned to explode in the upcoming decades.

Fruit Growers Enter Wine Market

Around the same time that Michigan vintners were expanding their grape varietals, some farmers began to take note of the new demand for wine grapes. Several fruit orchards were converted to vineyards in the late 1970s, one of which launched one of the state's largest wineries of today.

New Life for Cherry Orchards Becomes Leelanau Wine Cellars

Grand Rapids attorney Mike Jacobson bought a resort home in Northport, located on Leelanau Peninsula's most northern point. The home was situated within a three-hundred-acre cherry farm, making Mike an instant farmer. Mike hired Charles (Chuck) Kalchik to manage the operations of his new investment. This relationship turned into a partnership when the two acquired additional farm properties together, including orchards of more cherries and apples, peaches and other fruits. They also built a cherry-processing plant in Northport and created a local cooperative, which later merged into Cherry Growers, a grower-owned cooperative consisting of roughly one hundred growers.

To take advantage of the new demand for wine grapes, they converted ten acres of a cherry orchard in Suttons Bay into a French-American hybrid vineyard. The initial plantings took place in May 1974 and consisted of De Chaunac, Vignoles and Baco Noir. The vineyard expanded and was eventually replanted with all Baco Noir.

On April 18, 1975, Mike and Chuck established Leelanau Wine Cellars and released the first vintage in 1977. They purchased a vacant cherry-processing plant in Omena and converted it to a production facility to start the winery. The same year, they hired Nathan Stackhouse, who previously made wines for St. Julian Wine Company and Warner Vineyards in Paw Paw. Nathan was instrumental in setting up the initial facility and starting the production of winemaking that eventually led to the state's largest winery.

Multigenerational Farmer Opens Good Harbor Vineyards

Fruit farmer Bruce Simpson's agricultural roots date back to 1773, when his ancestors were first granted land in America. He began farming at the age of five on his family's three-hundred-acre cherry orchard. Upon graduating high school, he earned an agricultural degree at Michigan State University with plans to return to the family farm, though his dream was to open a winery. His grandfather agreed to finance Bruce's dream if he earned a degree in viticulture and enology at the University of California Davis.

Bruce returned to Leland in the late 1970s and converted fifteen acres of the family's farm to French-American hybrid and European vinifera grapevines as a third-generation grower on Leelanau Peninsula. He opened Good Harbor Vineyards in Leland in 1980. Early on, he teamed with Michigan State University to assist on research projects and provide land for testing various varietals.

Bruce preferred to produce wines with limited manipulation of the production process so that the land was expressed in the flavors of the wine. He strove to produce high-quality wines that people could afford. Two of his wines, the popular Trillium and Fishtown White, made up close to half of his total production.

Today, the winery produces fifteen thousand cases each year and processes wines for other state vintners. Sixty-seven acres of the family's farm are devoted to growing grapevines, including one of Michigan's largest Pinot Grigio plantings.

Bruce, who passed away in 2009, left a legacy of farming to his children, Sam and Taylor. Today, the brother-and-sister team manages the winery, and they continue their father's winemaking traditions while applying their business experiences to the company.

MICHIGAN STATE UNIVERSITY AND WINE GRAPE RESEARCH

Starting in 1970, Michigan State University launched an extensive research effort on wine grapes, around the same time that winemakers were diversifying the plantings of grape varietals in response to the changing marketplace. This effort was led by Dr. G. Stanley Howell, a native of Alabama, who started his career at MSU in the summer of 1969. Stan joined MSU as a horticulturalist to perform 50 percent research and 50 percent extension work on small fruits: strawberries, blueberries and grapes. He was intent on developing a research base of information for the Great Lakes region, reflecting its short growing season and challenging climate. Initially, his work entailed mostly varietal testing on strawberries and cultural research on blueberries, though the long-term viability of the grape juice industry was increasingly of interest.

Mature grapevines were in abundance in Michigan, primarily in Van Buren and Berrien Counties. Concord grapevines were most prevalent, with the remainder consisting of about 10 percent Niagara, 1 percent Delaware, less than 1 percent French-American hybrid varietals and only five acres of European vinifera varietals, for a total of twelve thousand acres of grapevines. Stan was intrigued with the study of these grapes and started working closely with juice grape growers and users in the southwest region.

It was in this bountiful, grape-growing region in southwest Michigan that Stan, doing blueberry fieldwork at the time, discovered a fully bearing Baco Noir vineyard at Bronte Champagne and Wines Company. Along with C.M. Hansen of MSU's Department of Agriculture Engineering, he stopped by Bronte, as C.M. had heard the winery was producing good sparkling wines.

Stan also found more French-American hybrids, including De Chaunac, Chelois, Aurore and Seyval. While visiting, winemaker Angelo Spinazze asked Stan if MSU, as a land grant institution focused on agriculture education and research, could help the state's wine grape growers—similar to what was being done in New York, Ohio, Pennsylvania and Canada.

Stan moved forward with wine grape research, including the production of experimental wines at MSU, after gaining support from MSU College of Agriculture and Natural Resources dean Dr. Lawrence Boger and Department of Horticulture chair Dr. John Carew.

Right from the start, Stan believed that the most effective research occurred in the field or, in this case, the vineyard. One of his favorite quotes was from Matthew 20:6-7, which Bernie Rick had shared with him: "Why stand ye here idle; go ye into the vineyard."

Stan knew it was equally important to produce wines from the grape varietals that had been proven to survive Michigan's cold climate and produce high-quality tasting wine that was economically sound. He crafted MSU's first experimental wine in 1971 under the Spartan Cellars label.

Wine was made from grapes grown at two MSU research sites, the Sodus Township farm and Tabor Hill Vineyards in Buchanan. Varietals included Vidal Blanc, Baco Noir, Chelois, Cascade, Vignoles, Seyval and the numbered Seibel selection S.10868.

Within five years, Stan's MSU work was fully focused on challenging grape cultivars, training vine systems and crop control to achieve the highest-quality grapes and processed quality. His research evolved through his work at MSU research stations, in prime grower vineyard sites and in challenging soils, like the mesoclimate on MSU's campus. His keen scientific focus on evaluating grape varietals in the vineyard—and in the cellar—led to the significant evolvement of viticulture at MSU. Stan earned the nickname "Dr. Grape" for devoting forty years of his career to Michigan's grape and wine industry.

Stan retired from MSU as professor and viticulturist emeritus on September 1, 2006. With more than three hundred published articles in grape and wine science and industry journals, he continues to apply science and data to decision-making principles and remains active with efforts to educate the next generation of grape and wine producers through the VESTA program (Viticulture Enology Science and Technology).

He is recognized as a leading wine grape researcher and has been invited by peers to speak on research topics in important wine-producing regions in the United States, Australia, New Zealand, Canada, Mexico, Switzerland, South Africa and Italy. He has received numerous awards, including a Merit Award in 2007 from the American Society Enology and Viticulture.

SURVIVAL OF THE FITTEST

Although research and new plantings of table wines were successfully taking place in the state, the 1970s were tumultuous times for Michigan's wineries. In 1972, the industry was nearly stomped out when the State of Michigan changed law 16A. The law increased the amount that wineries needed to pay farmers for grapes to receive a much-needed tax break. The requirement, which had changed six years prior from $55 to $85, was now $100 per ton. The tax-break allowed for a reduction of forty-six cents per gallon, provided the wine was 16 percent alcohol or less and was made from 75 percent Michigan-grown grapes.

Although the wineries fought hard against the increase via the Michigan Wine Institute, law 16A prevailed. The change shut down operations for a handful of Michigan wineries established in the 1930s, while others struggled over the ensuing years and through the 1980s before closing.

St. Julian Wine Company and Warner Vineyards were the only two 1930s-established wineries to survive. Their survival was credited to continuing their family's winemaking traditions, strengthening grower relations, planting new vineyards and producing table wines crafted with French-American hybrid grapes to complement their fruit-style wines. Survivalists and visionaries, the wineries' leaders fought through the 1970s and persevered.

Survival of St. Julian Wine Company

St. Julian began to work with its growers in the early 1970s to plant vineyards with hybrid wine grapes and focus on grape research in conjunction with Dr. G. Stanley Howell of MSU. During this time, St. Julian experienced a series of calamities causing new financial challenges for the winery. On May 24, 1972, a large portion of St. Julian's winery building was destroyed by fire. Thousands of gallons of wine in storage were covered by water from the fire hoses, and by law, the wine had to be destroyed.

More tragically, during this timeframe, Mariano Meconi lost all three children—Robert, Eugene and Julia, all of whom were winery executives— to health-related deaths.

On the edge of financial disaster, St. Julian struggled for several years waiting for the French-American hybrid grapevines to produce grapes, thus enabling the winery to transition from just dessert-style wines to a broader range of wines that included table wines. Fortunately, due to the fortitude of Mariano and his son-in-law, Paul Braganini, St. Julian regained its financial foothold in the marketplace in the subsequent years, persevering through the 1970s to become one of the state's largest wine producers of today.

A very notable product was launched in 1973, when the winery established its Solera cream sherry process using the Niagara grape. The first Solera cream sherry was produced in 1975, using sherry wines made over the previous two vintages. St. Julian's Solera process comprised three "stages" and resulted in a total of just under twenty thousand gallons. The Solera system was set up as a stack of barrels, which internally acted as an intricate and fractional blending operation. Every bottle of St. Julian Solera cream sherry was a blend of sherry wines from every vintage, starting with the 1973 vintage and ending four years prior to the year of any given bottling. Today, Solera cream sherry is St. Julian's most award-winning product in the winery's history.

The centennial year of 1976 marked milestones for St. Julian. The winery celebrated "bottle number four million" of Cream D'or on October 22 at 9:30 a.m. St. Julian's new facility, reconstructed after the fire, was dedicated to Mariano's three children.

Michigan governor William Milliken awarded St. Julian with the State of Michigan's 1976 Ambassadors of Tours Award in recognition of the winery's long-standing leadership role in winery tourism. Two years later, Mariano's grandson, David Braganini, was named general manager and president of St. Julian. He continues to manage the family business today. Old schoolmate Charles "Chas" Catherman joined St. Julian in 1973, the same year David returned to his family's winery to work. Chas assumed winemaking duties in 1974, and remained with St. Julian for the next thirty-four years before retiring.

Survival of Michigan Wineries (Warner Vineyards)

John Turner's son-in-law, James K. Warner, who became president of the winery in 1951, was managing all elements of the winery and was responsible for new developments. James K. purchased the Village of Paw Paw's 1898 waterworks building along the Paw Paw River and converted the historic building into the Wine Haus tasting room in 1967. Three years earlier, John had passed away.

In these early years, vineyards flourished near the winery, making crop delivery for processing easier. Another step to simplify harvesting occurred when the Warners were among the first to use the new mechanical grape picker, which arrived in Michigan for the first time in 1968.

In 1969, James K. initiated the acquisition of Hommel Wine Company of Sandusky, Ohio, a major sparkling wine producer founded in 1878. The Warners began using the 1890 *méthode champenoise* equipment to produce Warner Vineyards' *Brut* Champagne, which earned the winery many accolades in ensuing years. It was produced with a blend of grapes, including Aurora Blanc.

By 1970, Michigan Wineries had become Michigan's largest winery. John's grandson, Bill Warner, shared, "Michigan Wineries was, at one time, four times larger than all the wineries combined in Michigan and the largest winery in the Midwest."

James J. Warner, John Turner's eldest Warner grandson, joined the winery and became executive vice-president in 1970. Around this time, the Warners were instrumental in providing a $15,000 grant to Dr. G. Stanley Howell of Michigan State University to convince MSU that the industry was serious about improving wine quality and believed MSU was the best "agent" for achieving this goal.

Along with backing MSU research, the Warners consulted with other experts. They visited the New York State Agricultural Experiment Station in Geneva and the Vineland Research Station in Ontario to research French-American hybrids, experiences that prompted the Warners to proceed with extensive plantings of these varietals, including Seyval, Aurora Blanc and Marechal Foch.

On July 1, 1973, Michigan Wineries became Warner Vineyards to honor the family's generations of winemaking. President Gerald Ford served Warner's *Brut* Champagne at the White House that year. The Warner family continues to produce the sparkling wine today using the in-bottle fermentation process.

Also in 1973, the Warners hired Richard Vine, who stayed with Warner Vineyards for four years. The winery began an extensive planting program that included plantings of estate vineyards and additional vineyards under contract. By the mid-1970s, the Warners had eighty-nine acres of French-American hybrids planted as part of their total five hundred acres of grapevines. Warner credited Dick with initiating the production of Solera cream sherry and positioning the winery in the table wine business. Dick encouraged the planting of more hybrid grapes and established a vine nursery. He was also instrumental in convincing longtime juice grape growers to plant French-American hybrids on their farmland. Dick later established a wine education and appreciation program at Purdue University.

At the same time, the Warners continued to grow in the private label grape juice and concentrate business, utilizing the significant amount of Concord grapes in the region. At one time, Warner was providing grape juice for fifty to sixty private label grape juice companies—including for Very Fine Juices' eight-ounce bottles—and operating three shifts from its Paw Paw Grape Juice facility. Grape juice accounted for several million dollars a year in business and eventually became an even bigger business for the family than wine. At the winery's peak, Warner Vineyards' annual sales exceeded $7,500,000, and it employed 125 people.

Eventually, though, Warner Vineyards began to experience operational difficulties. A culmination of difficult events caused a financial downturn for the winery. In 1990, James J. left the unprofitable juice-packing business, which employed 80 of his 105 employees.

A retooling of the business led James J. to consult with William Welsch of Fenn Valley Vineyards while the two served as board members of the Michigan Grape and Wine Industry Council. Today, Warner Vineyards wines are crafted by Doug Welsch and consist of 100 percent grapes and other fruits—including blueberries, cherries and peaches—grown within the Lake Michigan Shore appellation. The Warner family is focused on opening tasting rooms in key tourism areas to reach new customers.

VINTNERS ENVISION THE FUTURE

The new plantings of grape varietals in the 1960s and 1970s strengthened Michigan's acreage of wine grapes. The surviving wineries continued to retool their operations to be in a better position to serve the changing marketplace in the next era. Entering the 1980s, Michigan's vintners were passionately pursuing their visions for table wines reflective of Michigan's maritime climate and fruit wines that conveyed Michigan's agricultural bounty.

AGRICULTURAL BOUNTY

1980 to 2010

G lacial movements several thousand years ago formed two large peninsulas surrounded by massive lakes. Michigan's peninsulas consist of diverse terrains, including rolling moraines, dense forests, coastal dunes and inland lakes and rivers. Our soils vary from towering sand dunes to sandy loam, silt, clay, gravel, bedrock and mineral rich soils—and, sometimes, a sporadic combination of them all.

An ideal wine grape vineyard site is on a south-sloping hillside with maximum sun exposure and fertile, well-drained loam soils. With this said, many of our winemakers have found other soil mixes that benefit their style of winemaking. And, truly, it's more than land that influences our wines. Air, water and weather intermingle and aid, or often hinder, winemakers on their quest to perfect their wines. Many elements come together to impart characteristics into wines to express a sense of place or distinct origin—or, as the French say, *terroir*. When it all comes together, it's exquisite.

Michigan has four defined seasons, though the most prevailing influential factor is lake effect, created by the massive fresh waters of the Great Lakes, particularly Lake Michigan. Prevailing westerly winds moderate seasonal temperatures, cooling the air in the summer and warming the air in the fall. This climate buffer extends the warmer growing season along Michigan's west coast, creating a burgeoning fruit belt where grapes and other fruits thrive.

The plantings of new varietals in the 1960s and 1970s and product evolution in the forthcoming years relied heavily on Michigan's *terroir*, climate, lake effect and, above all, winemakers' skills and ability to respond to the marketplace.

At the start of the early 1980s, the skills of our winemakers were put into play, perhaps more so than in any other time in history to date. Annual wine production was at an all-time low of 250,000 cases. Two more of Michigan's wineries closed due to declining consumer demand, particularly for sweeter wines with higher alcohol. Overall wine sales were down in the state; still, table-style wine production was on the rise. With French-American hybrid and European vinifera grapevines flourishing, the foundation of Michigan's contemporary wine industry was settling into place. However, as the industry struggled through these changes, it became apparent that funding was needed to continue research on grape varietals that thrived in Michigan and to promote the industry.

MICHIGAN GRAPE AND WINE INDUSTRY COUNCIL

In response to the need for further research, the Michigan Grape and Wine Industry Council (MGWIC) was established as a program of the Department of Agriculture in 1985. At the time the council was formed, Michigan had fifteen commercial wineries and 10,800 acres of vineyards, of which 875 acres were dedicated to wine production.

The council's main objectives are to provide research, education and promotion for the Michigan grape and wine industry. In 1986, the first full year of the council, nearly $83,000 was funded for research on Michigan wine grapes and wines. Since then, the council has funded more than $2,500,000 in research in the first twenty-five years of its existence. Significant funding has been applied to research in collaboration with Michigan State University.

Additional emphasis is placed on increasing vineyard acreage in the state to keep up with demand. Under the direction of program manager Linda Jones, the council assists growers in selecting the appropriate varietals to plant.

"Growers can make educated decisions about what varieties to grow by reviewing viticultural and consumer research, the experiences of other wineries in Michigan and beyond and evaluating this information in the context of their business model and their own viticultural experience on a particular vineyard site," says Linda.

Besides funding research, the council also hosts the annual Michigan Wine and Spirits Competition, an annual conference for industry members, and has directed promotional programs for the industry since its establishment. A flagship of the council's promotional effort is an annual four-color, glossy *Michigan Wine Country* magazine, first published in 1999. The purpose of the magazine is to share news of developments and activities within the various wine regions of Michigan and to promote Michigan wines to consumers. Since its establishment, the council has been an industry asset. Around the time the council was started, four American Viticultural Areas were designated in the state.

American Viticultural Areas

During the 1980s, specific growing regions in Michigan were acknowledged as wine grape–growing areas. New federal regulations mandated vital changes on how wines could legally be labeled. To note the wine's vintage—the year the grape was harvested—the wine grape had to be grown within a federally designated wine grape–growing region. The same rules applied for labeling a wine as estate-bottled. These federally designated regions were called American Viticultural Areas, or more simply, AVAs.

Very often, AVAs are confused with appellations, or the two terms are used loosely when referring to one or the other. An AVA is a designated wine grape–growing region approved and established through the Alcohol and Tobacco Tax and Trade Bureau (TTB), formerly the Bureau of Alcohol, Tobacco, Firearms and Explosives (ATFE).

The geographical area is petitioned, most likely by a vintner, for approval and is defined by specific geographical boundaries. In order for a vintner to list an AVA on the wine label, at least 85 percent of the grapes used to produce the wine must be grown within the geographical area, as defined by law.

An appellation, on the other hand, is a protected name under which a wine may be labeled. It's a geographical indication of where the grapes are grown. The rules that govern appellations are dependent on the country in which the wine is produced. These specifications can include, but are not limited to, what varieties of grapes may be grown, maximum grape yields, alcohol level and other quality factors. The state of Michigan, as a whole, is an appellation.

With the evolution of Americans' preferences for wines that express a place of origin, Michigan's vintners felt that AVA designations were necessary. The ability to list the AVA on their wine labels was important to the overall marketing and branding of their wines. The AVAs allowed the vintner to denote the uniqueness of the region in which the wines were produced. Several of Michigan's vintners petitioned the TTB to get their growing regions designated, which eventually resulted in four AVAs, all of which are located near the west coast of the Lower Peninsula along the shores of Lake Michigan.

Fennville AVA

Fennville is the first AVA in Michigan, and the third in the United States, following Augusta (Missouri) and Napa Valley. Located in southwest Michigan, it was established on September 18, 1981. Fenn Valley Vineyards is and always has been the only commercial winery located within the AVA. The petition was initiated by the Welsch family, owners of the winery, after a long struggle between other wineries in southwest Michigan over what boundaries should be established and which wineries should be included. The Fennville AVA consists of seventy-five thousand acres and is completely located within the boundaries of the Lake Michigan Shore AVA. It is mostly located in the southwest portion of Allegan County, with a small section extending into the northwest corner of Van Buren County.

Leelanau Peninsula AVA

Michigan's second AVA is Leelanau Peninsula, located in northwest Michigan and established on March 30, 1982. The peninsula's vintners deemed the AVA necessary to continue to label their wines as estate-bottled. The Leelanau Peninsula AVA is the same size as the Fennville AVA, at seventy-five thousand acres, and includes all of Leelanau County except for the offshore islands of North and South Manitou Islands.

Lake Michigan Shore AVA

Located in southwest Michigan, Lake Michigan Shore became the state's third AVA after its establishment on October 13, 1983. Consisting of 1,280,000 acres, it is by far the state's largest AVA, larger than the other three areas combined. It is located in the southwest corner of the state, seventy-two miles along the shores of Lake Michigan. From the north, it starts at the Kalamazoo River's intersection with Lake Michigan and then winds its way along the river about thirty-five miles until it intersects the Penn Central Railroad line just south of the city of Otsego. The east border travels south along the Penn Central Railroad line and through the city of Kalamazoo for about twenty-five miles until it intersects the Grand Trunk Western Railroad line in Schoolcraft. It then traverses southwest along the railroad about thirty-five miles to the state border. After about thirty-eight miles running along the border, it connects to Lake Michigan and completes the defined region.

Old Mission Peninsula AVA

The Old Mission Peninsula AVA was established on June 8, 1987. Old Mission Peninsula, located in northwest Michigan, is Michigan's smallest AVA, consisting of only 19,200 acres. The defined area is all of Peninsula Township, excluding the offshore islands of Marion and Bassett Islands, and a small portion of Traverse City Township.

In comparison, the Napa Valley AVA is forty-three thousand acres consisting of more than three hundred wineries. This is a little more than double the size of Old Mission Peninsula, with seven wineries, and just over half the size of both Fennville and Leelanau Peninsula, with only one and eighteen wineries, respectively. Lake Michigan Shore, with its massive acreage of 1,280,000, hosts fifteen wineries.

Beyond the AVAs

It's important to note that not all of Michigan's wineries are located within AVAs, and wine grapes growing in other regions of the state are flourishing and producing high-quality wines. Mesoclimates can provide ideal growing conditions to inland vineyards. As needed, some inland wineries supplement their crops with grapes from growers of vineyards located within twenty-five miles of the Lake Michigan shoreline.

SPARKLING PAST...SPARKLING FUTURE

Since the 1940s, Michigan sparkling wines have garnered notoriety on a national basis. Bronte Champagne and Cold Duck were hot sellers in tasting rooms, markets and restaurants. Bronte's Cold Duck was the inspiration for E.J. Gallo Winery to launch the still very popular line of Andre wines. In the late 1940s, St. Julian produced its first sparkling wine before venturing into nonalcoholic sparkling juices, which are gaining market share beyond Michigan today. At Warner Vineyards, sparkling wine production was ignited with the purchase of 1800s-era *méthode champenoise* equipment from an old winery in Ohio. Warner's *Brut* Champagne was named Agricultural Product of the Year and was served at two Super Bowls and also in the White House. Tabor Hill Winery and L. Mawby Vineyards launched sparkling wine production in the 1980s, garnering awards and notoriety for their bubblies. By the 1990s, Larry Mawby had become the first Michigan vintner to focus solely on the production of sparkling wines.

Michigan's Sparkling Wine Leader: L. Mawby Vineyards

Larry Mawby, one of three vintners to initiate the Leelanau Peninsula AVA designation, began growing a smorgasbord of grape varieties in 1973 on a former thirty-two-acre strawberry and hay farm in Suttons Bay. He established L. Mawby Vineyards in 1978, opening a winery and tasting room three years later. In 1984, he added the production of sparkling wines to his still wine production, eventually garnering a reputation as an expert in sparkling wines.

When making the decision to specialize in sparkling wines, Larry did not reflect on the success of Michigan's sparkling wine history of the 1950s and 1960s. Instead, he considered climate conditions of the renowned Champagne region of France, which relatively compared to the conditions of his own property on the forty-fifth parallel in northern Michigan. His immediate focus was *méthode champenoise*, the traditional process of developing sparkling wines, first developed in the Champagne region. With this method, wine undergoes a second fermentation in the bottle to create a more complex wine.

The L. Mawby label wines are crafted from grapes grown on his estate and elsewhere on the peninsula. His customers reacted favorably, and in response, he created a bold second label, M. Lawrence, in 2003 to increase production volume using the Charmat, or bulk, method, where a second fermentation takes place in the tanks. Larry calls this his *"cuvée* close" method. This process requires less aging, which allows Larry to produce more and offer it to consumers at a more affordable price point.

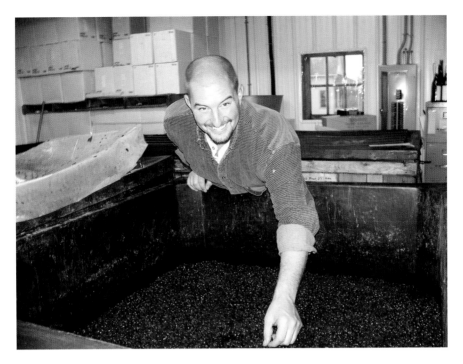

Winemaker Mike De Schaaf of Hickory Creek Winery in Baroda.

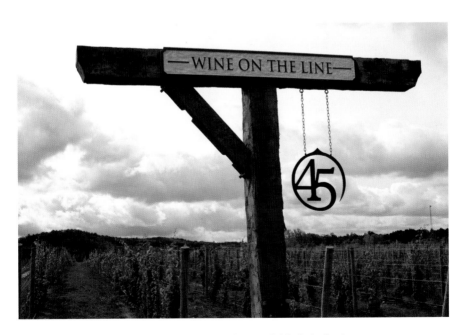

45 North Vineyard and Winery on the forty-fifth parallel in Lake Leelanau.

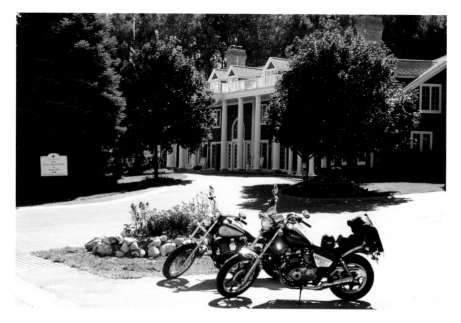

Escape to The Inn at Black Star Farms in Suttons Bay.

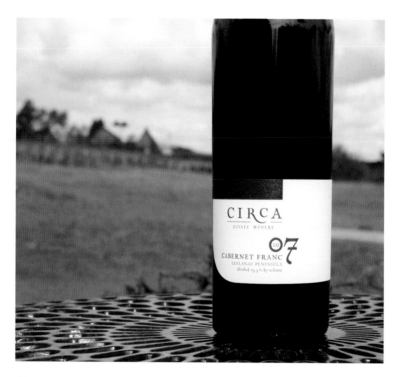

Circa Estate Winery 2007 Cabernet Franc on Leelanau Peninsula.

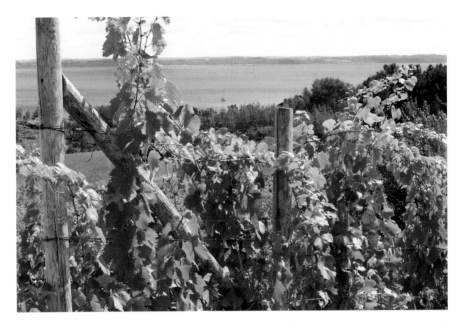

Willow Vineyard in Suttons Bay features a magnificent million-dollar view.

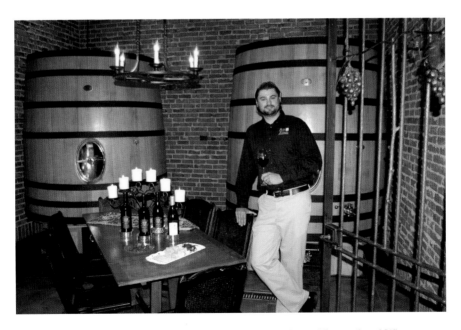

Winemaker Coenraad Stassen in the barrel room of Brys Estate Vineyard and Winery on Old Mission Peninsula. *Courtesy of Brys Estate Vineyard and Winery.*

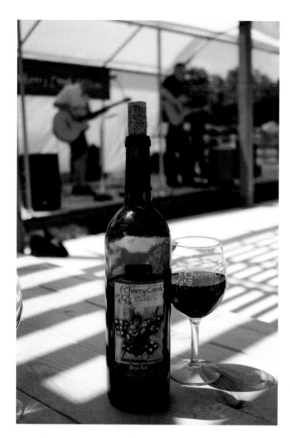

Left: Summertime music at Cherry Creek Cellars in the Irish Hills region of southeast Michigan.

Below: David Braganini points to his grandfather, Mariano Meconi, founder of the family's St. Julian Wine Company.

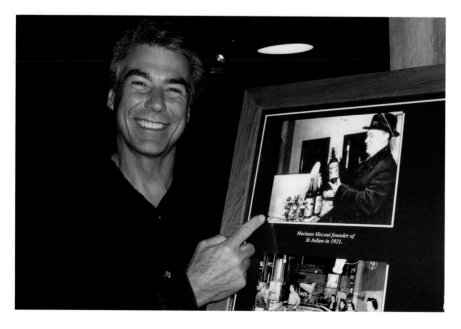

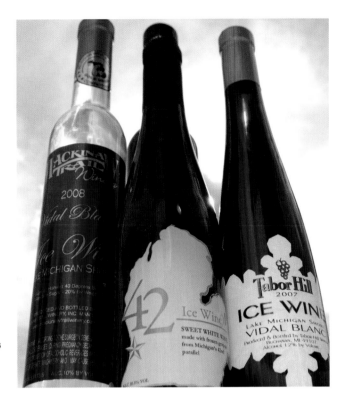

Michigan ice wine intensely concentrates flavors reflective of the Great Lakes maritime climate.

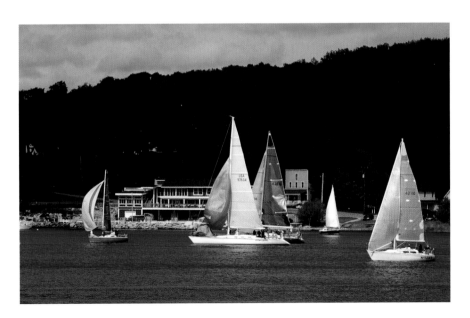

A sailboat regatta in front of the Leelanau Cellars tasting room on Lake Michigan. *Photograph by Jim Miller.*

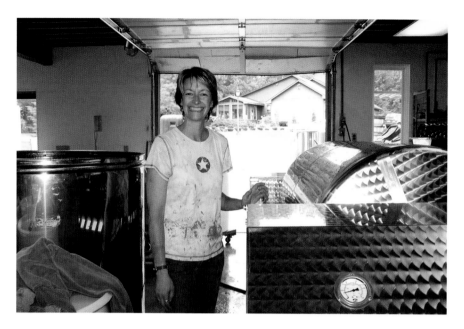

Winemaker Holly Balansag of Sandhill Crane Vineyards of Jackson.

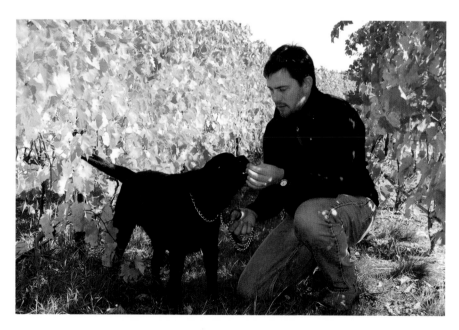

Winemaker Lee Lutes of Black Star Farms with Bear in Suttons Bay vineyard.

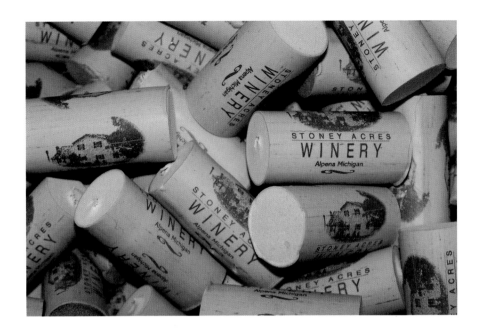

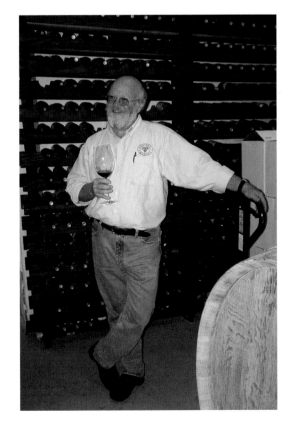

Above: Stoney Acres Winery uncorked in Alpena.

Right: Winemaker Mark Johnson of Chateau Chantal on Old Mission Peninsula.

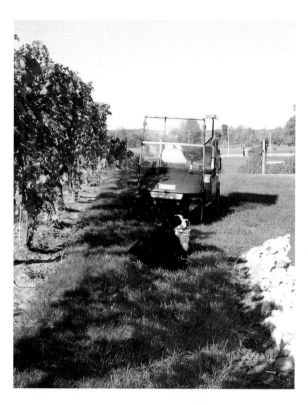

Left: Tee up along the vines at Bowers Harbor Vineyards on Old Mission Peninsula.

Below: Brothers Matt Moersch and Chris Moersch of Round Barn Winery and Free Run Cellars of southwest Michigan. *Courtesy of Round Barn Winery.*

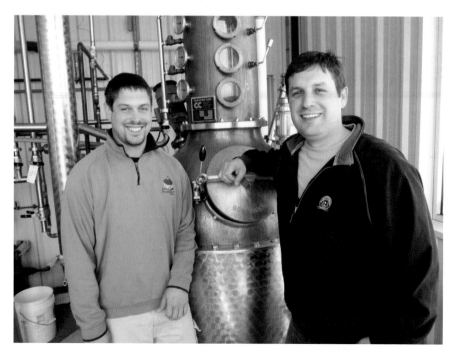

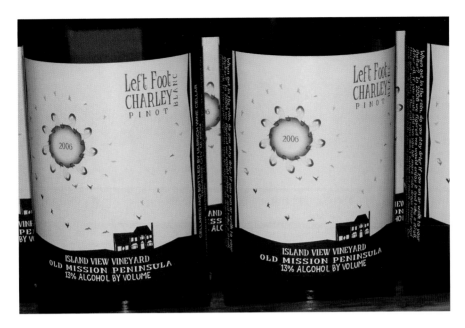

Left Foot Charley 2006 Pinot Blanc in Traverse City.

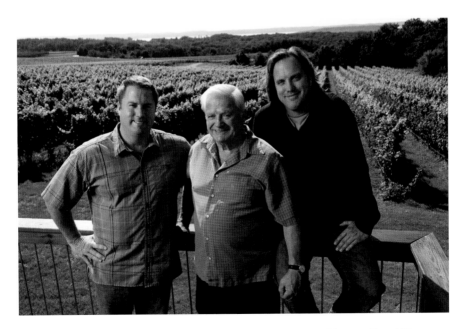

Ed O'Keefe III, Ed O'Keefe and Sean O'Keefe of family-owned Chateau Grand Traverse on Old Mission Peninsula. *Photograph by Don Rutt.*

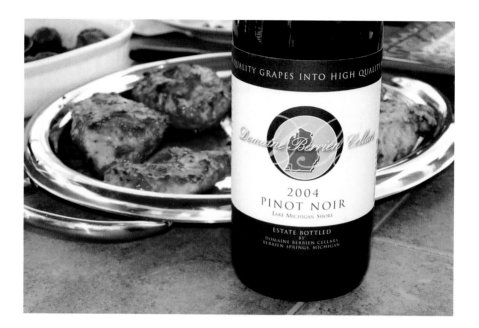

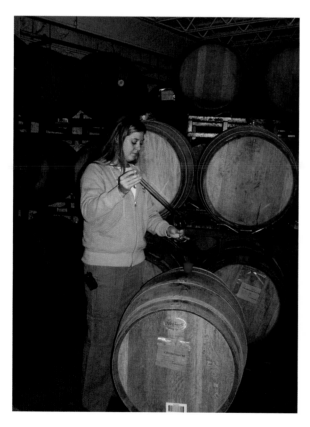

Above: Domaine Berrien Cellars 2004 Pinot Noir paired with grilled barbecue chicken.

Left: Winemaker Nancie Corum tastes a barrel sample at St. Julian Wine Company of Paw Paw.

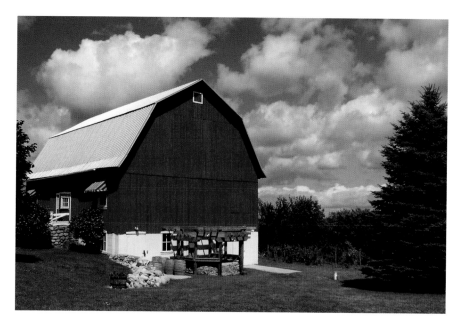

Ciccone Vineyard and Winery's 1937 renovated barn in Suttons Bay.

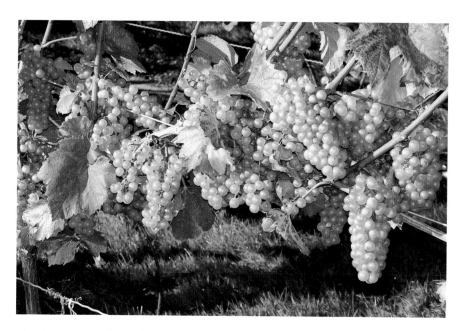

Chardonnay grapevines at Bowers Harbor Vineyards on Old Mission Peninsula.

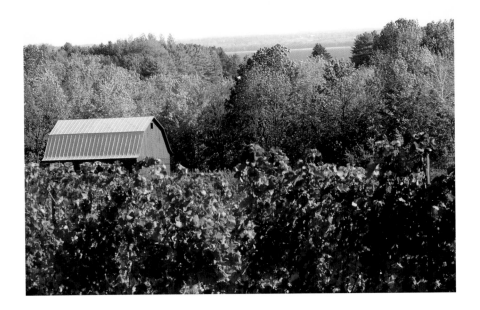

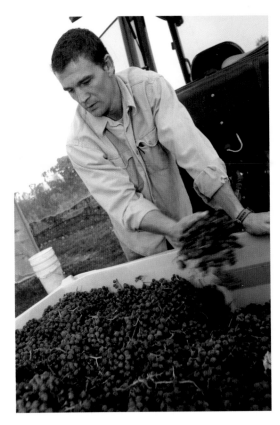

Above: Brys Estate Vineyard and Winery's vineyard and barn overlooking Grand Traverse Bay on Old Mission Peninsula.

Left: Winemaker Cornel Olivier of 2 Lads Winery on Old Mission Peninsula sorting grapes at harvest. *Photograph by Paul Osborne.*

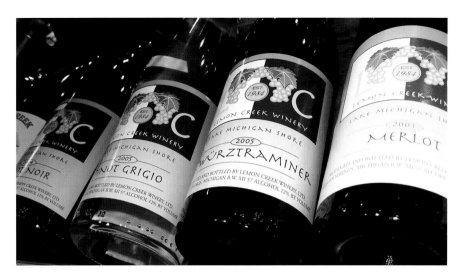

Lemon Creek Winery wine selection at Berrien Springs.

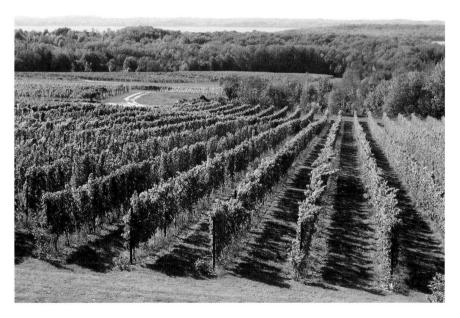

Autumn vineyards of Chateau Grand Traverse overlooking Grand Traverse Bay on Old Mission Peninsula.

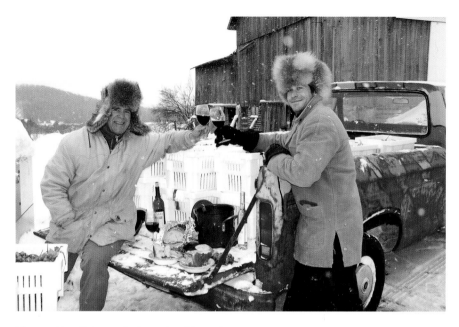

Vintner Alan Eaker and winemaker Shawn Walters toast to a successful ice wine harvest at Longview Winery on Leelanau Peninsula.

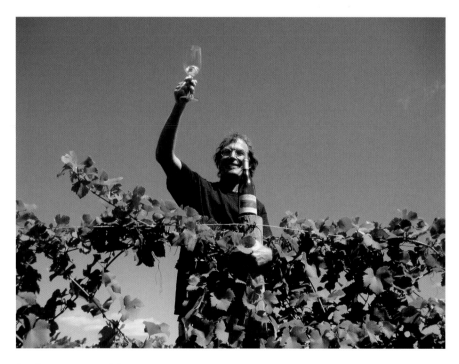

Dr. Charlie Edson of Bel Lago Vineyard and Winery in Cedar overlooking Lake Leelanau.

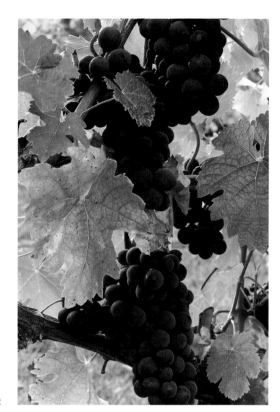

Right: Pinot Noir grapes ready for harvest.

Below: Stay overnight at stunning Chateau Chantal on Old Mission Peninsula. *Photograph by Brian Confer.*

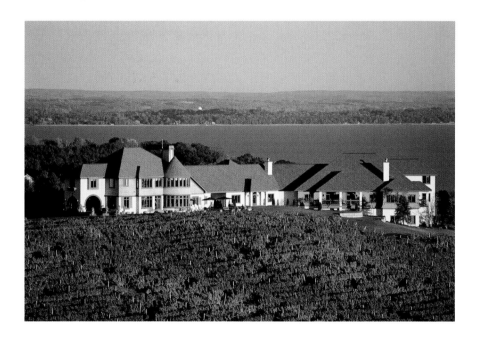

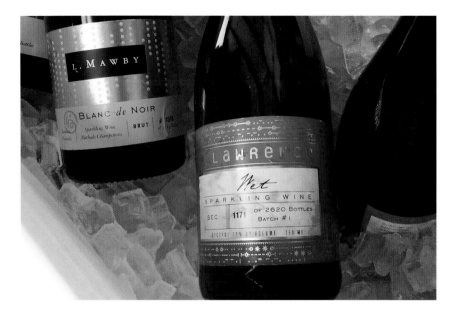

L. Mawby sparkling wines.

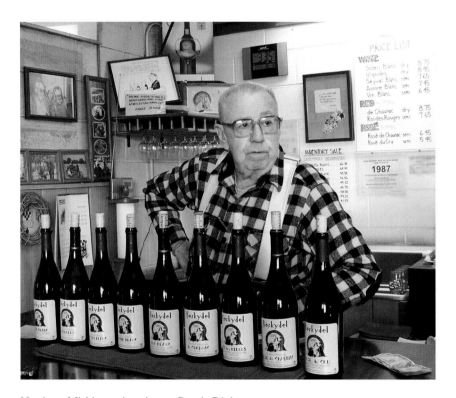

Northern Michigan wine pioneer Bernie Rink.

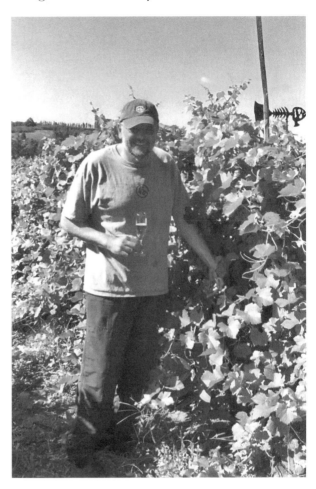

Sparkling wine advocate
Larry Mawby in his L.
Mawby vineyards in
Suttons Bay.

Larry's success can be partly attributed to his encouragement of celebrating everyday moments, not just special occasions, with sparkling wine. Michigan's sparkling wine leader of today knows this to be true, as his business keeps booming since he made the gutsy decision to focus solely on sparkling wine production during the 1990s.

Today's signature wines include Blanc de Blanc, which Larry says expresses the idiosyncrasies of Leelanau Peninsula and is chiefly made with Chardonnay. His most popular sparkling wine is Sex, which clearly communicates his fun attitude about enjoying the wine and the moment. Together, these two wines equal nearly half of the winery's production. Sandpiper, another top seller, exemplifies a mosaic of all the wines entering the wine facility each year.

"It's very approachable, reasonably priced and fun, and we only sell it at the winery," states Larry.

After years of market demand exceeding production, Larry sought a new partner in Stuart Laing in 2009. Now, the winery is set up to produce eighteen thousand cases annually. Notably, Larry and Stuart donated the thirty-two-acre vineyard as an easement to the Leelanau Conservancy to permanently protect the vineyard from development. The Leelanau Conservancy is a nonprofit organization created to protect, preserve and conserve the land and water resources of Leelanau County.

An exciting 2010 release is Detroit, a new M. Lawrence blend of Riesling, Traminette and Cayuga. Larry feels that the bubbly honors Detroiters. He is excited to give them a wine to toast everyday celebrations.

Larry's niche in sparkling wine production in Michigan garnered the winemaker and his wines national attention. Even renowned chef Mario Batali is a fan. He tasted L. Mawby sparkling wine at a benefit dinner for the Leelanau Conservancy and called the wine "remarkable and world class."

While Larry was igniting his sparkling wine business, other vintners in the state took the effervescent plunge and produced standout wines.

Tabor Hill Winery: A Toast to Visionaries

In Michigan's southwest corner in Buchanan, Tabor Hill Winery was embarking on the development of a sparkling wine program around the same time as L. Mawby's foray into bubblies. Since 1979, David Upton, who passed away in 2009, was proprietor of Tabor Hill Winery. Born and raised in the area, David knew that the farmland is as fertile here as anywhere in the world and believed grapes can grow as well in the soil as other fruits and vegetables that have been growing in the region for decades.

In the fall of 1979, Rick Moersch, a local high school biology teacher, was recruited to help solve a spoilage problem in the winery. He analyzed the problems, provided a solution and was immediately hired on a part-time basis. While applying his experience to the challenges of winemaking, he was in his element, soaking up as much knowledge as he could. He read books, visited wineries and vineyards and, by spring, was hired on a full-time basis. Rick was hooked on winemaking, and in 1981, he planted his own vineyard.

Also in 1979, Mike Merchant was hired to work in the cellar and vineyard after graduating from Michigan State University's soil sciences and wine grape management program under Dr. G. Stanley Howell.

Incidentally, in 1981, Bob Hope, became a huge fan of Tabor Hill's Vidal Blanc Demi-Sec after first receiving it at a Berrien County Youth Fair. He performed at the fair and was given a bottle of wine during his performance. In later years, he often flew into southwest Michigan, or arranged for someone to fly in, to pick up cases of his favorite Tabor Hill wine.

In 1984, David acquired Bronte Champagne and Wines Company's equipment under a bulk sales act and hired Bronte's winemaker, Angelo Spinazze, as a consultant. With the transferring of the equipment, Rick was able to dispel the Prohibition-era rumor that one of Bronte's tanks was riddled with bullet holes from Al Capone. As Rick explained, "They are drainage holes."

Tabor Hill began to focus on producing quality wines by growing the existing French-American hybrid vines well and planning for future vinifera vineyards. Along with his wife, Linda, David focused on creating a vineyard destination for sampling regional wines and foods.

In 1986, Rick and David decided to create a platform for world-class vintage sparkling wines. Rick recruited renowned French winemaker Claude Thibaut, who consulted with him over a five-year period. Tabor Hill rented *méthode champenoise* equipment from Doug Welsch of Fenn Valley Vineyards, paying a $2.50 per case fee to make Tabor Hill's vintage Grand Mark sparkling wine. The bubbly quickly garnered praise. Tabor Hill's Grand Mark is one of the heritage wines that the winery still produces today.

In 1992, Rick left Tabor Hill to open his own winery, now called Round Barn Winery. Rick's experience with sparkling wine production fired an interest in different styles of production, which came into play in the late 1990s when Michigan's micro distilling law changed and enabled wineries to produce fruit-based brandies. Mike Merchant took over the winemaking duties at Tabor Hill and continues to lead wine production and manage the vineyard.

By 2007, a nine-thousand-square-foot expansion was added to the warehouse to accommodate the growing production and inventory, which, by 2008, had reached sixty-five thousand cases a year. The winery's classic Demi-Sec continues to be the top seller, though perhaps the most honorable wine at Tabor Hill is the Spumante, launched as a tribute to winemaker Angelo Spinazze, who left behind a remarkable legacy in Michigan's wine industry.

Dazzling Black Star Farms

Black Star Farms is a striking estate that reflects bygone eras. An elegant inn, artisan cheese handcrafted by Leelanau Cheese Company and wood-fired pizzas prepared with fresh, seasonal ingredients in the casual café make Black Star Farms a perfect day or overnight destination. Horses graze in the lush, green fields. Forests surround the valley where the estate is tucked away in the countryside of Suttons Bay on Leelanau Peninsula. A breadth of wines and other specialty drinks are offered in the wide-open tasting room. Notably, the sparkling wine dazzles.

The winery opened in 1999 as a shared vision by proprietors Don Coe, local grower Kerm Campbell and winemaker Lee Lutes to create a business where they could grow value-added agriculture and demonstrate farming as an active, viable business. "Our vision is to connect wine with the land," states Don. "Wine is produced from a vine rooted in the vineyard—it doesn't just appear on supermarket shelves." The winery produces more than thirty wines and seven distilled spirits.

In 1998, winemaker Lee Lutes produced the winery's first sparkling wine, with the help of disgorging equipment from neighboring winemaker Larry Mawby. For the first two years, he used the traditional *méthode champenoise* process, launching Blanc de Blanc. "We're very fond of sparkling wine and are committed to using high-caliber fruit," says Lee. It's for this reason that the winery laid off sparkling wine production for a few years while seeking top-quality fruit for future vintages. In 2004, production resumed, resulting in five hundred cases of quality bubbly.

In 2007, Lee released a tank-fermented sparkling wine that was softer on the palate with toned down acidity and breadiness. He described the wine as "casual, fruit-forward and easy drinking; fresh and tooty-fruity." The wine was named Be Dazzled and quickly bedazzled customers, convincing Lee to ramp up production of this customer-friendly sparkler. Production is expected to grow from one thousand to two thousand cases annually for this fun bubbly, which blends Pinot Noir and Chardonnay with smaller doses of Pinot Gris and Pinot Blanc.

In 2010, the winery produced a Blanc de Noir, a 100 percent Pinot Noir classic-style sparkling wine that is softer in acidity, richer on the palate and yeasty. This bubbly is a reflection of the style of classic French Champagne. It will likely be released in 2012.

Sparkling Terroir: *2 Lads Winery*

Near the tip of Old Mission Peninsula in Traverse City, 2 Lads Winery sits atop a stunning hillside basking amid the West and East Bays of Lake Michigan. The winery opened in 2007 with a unique tasting room and winemaking facility like no other in the state. Cool-climate reds and sparkling wines are the focus, though small batches of white wines are produced.

Vintner Chris Baldyga, one of the two lads, feels the *terroir* surrounding their gleaming tasting room is ideal for the varietals for sparkling wine. The other lad, winemaker Cornel Olivier, immigrated to the United States from South Africa, where he learned winemaking from his grandfather and earned a degree in viticulture and wine science from Elsenburg Agricultural College. Before opening 2 Lads with Chris, he was an award-winning winemaker of Brys Estate Vineyard and Winery located a few miles down the road.

Chris and Cornel source their grapes from twenty-two acres of estate grapevines and three additional acres at Chris's personal homestead on the peninsula.

"We have a strong sense of place in our wines," shares Chris.

> *Our vineyard naturally sits atop a lot of clay and loam, and it's even mixed with rock and gravel. We use a vineyard spader to turn beneficial cover crops into the soils twice a year, so you get a lot of natural fiber and green mass for heartier soils. Our wines reflect our unique sense of place and are a definite reflection of our* terroir. *Everything tastes fuller with distinct, expressive flavors.*

In the spring of 2007, the vintners had the opportunity to acquire *méthode champenoise* equipment, previously owned by L. Mawby Vineyards and then by Chateau Grand Traverse. The new winery owners jumped at the chance to pursue a sparkling wine production program in their facility.

"We love making sparkling wine, and we're really good at it," says Chris. "Pinot Noir, Chardonnay, Riesling and Pinot Grigio provide the premium fruit for the style of sparkling wine most Americans prefer, which is more fruit-forward, clean and bright."

For those who prefer classic sparkling wine reflective of traditional French Champagne, 2 Lads is producing a Pinot Noir and Chardonnay blend that has been aging for several years with a possible release in 2013.

Chris and Cornel believe in letting the *terroir* speak for itself. "Each vintage will dictate the blend for the sparkling wines we produce," says Chris.

Michigan's Future May Sparkle Brighter

In 2007, Dr. Paolo Sabbatini joined MSU as assistant professor of horticulture to continue the research and extension that Dr. G. Stanley Howell initiated more than three decades ago. Paolo earned a master's degree and PhD in horticulture at Italy's University of Ancona before immigrating to the United States in 2004 for his postdoctorate work. His native city of Jesi, located in the Marche region of Italy, is renowned for its Verdicchio grapes.

At MSU, Paolo has focused on viticulture, and more specifically, identifying environmental, physiological and cultural factors that limit growth and development of the vines and the maturity and quality of the fruit. His ultimate research goal is to optimize the productivity and quality of grapes. To achieve his goal, he works closely with team members at the university's Southwest Michigan Research and Extension Center in Berrien County and Northwest Michigan Horticultural Research Station in Grand Traverse County.

As a land grant institute, MSU's focus on varietal testing is paramount. Essentially, the institution is bearing the costs of trials rather than having growers taking risks with their crops. The college is currently testing fifty varietals in test plots on campus and at the research stations. Cultivars of particular interest include Marsanne, Roussane, Valvin muscat, Gruner veltliner and Zweigelt.

Paolo has also planted the Italian grape, Prosecco, on campus, possibly the first planting of this grape in the United States. Prosecco is from the Veneto region of Italy, where is it used in sparkling and still wines. Paolo believes that this grape, as well as others from Italy planted in the trial—Teroldego and Tocai friuliano—can play an important role in the evolution of Michigan's sparkling wine industry.

"Sparkling wine is definitely part of our *terroir*," affirms Paolo. MSU is planting cuttings at the regional research centers in Benton Harbor and in Traverse City, though the testing results won't be known for several years. If all grows well, expect to find sparkling Prosecco in Michigan's future.

On a related note, Paolo, along with Dr. Tom Zabadal, MSU professor and coordinator of the Southwest Michigan Research and Extension Center, are leading a multistate variety trial in conjunction with fifteen other states called Coordinated Wine Grape Variety Evaluations in the Eastern USA.

Variety testing at twenty-five sites, including Michigan's two research sites, was established in the spring of 2008. The project will conclude in 2017, and data collected during these trials will be evaluated and shared among the states. This data will be invaluable to vintners and growers in Michigan and beyond and will be instrumental in laying the groundwork for the plantings of additional wine grape vineyards.

From Fruit Orchards to Wine Grape Vineyards

As with all commodities, markets evolve and customer demand and supply changes from year to year. In the fruit industry, supply is also challenged by fickle Mother Nature. Depending on her mood, Mother Nature adversely affects fruit supply or pumps up seasonal volumes.

During the 1980s, Michigan's cherry industry sought diversification to expand beyond its existing market. Tart cherries were largely grown for processing, as opposed to sweet cherries, which serve the fresh market. The Cherry Marketing Institute, a national organization, was launched in 1987 in Lansing to develop new ideas to market the cherry. Interestingly, Michigan's commercial cherry industry was planted nearly the same time as the wine industry in the late 1800s.

As the wine industry slowly rebuilt itself with the planting of new varietals, Michigan fruit farmers took note, including a few cherry farmers. They followed the lead of Leelanau Wine Cellars and Good Harbor Vineyards in the 1970s, reviving cherry farms with the plantings of vines.

Unlike grapevines that can flourish for decades, some cherry tree varieties are aged after twenty-five years. The planting of new cherry trees is significantly less costly than the planting of wine grapes. However, year-round tourism is an attractive selling point to some farmers, who began to tear out old orchards and replace them with vineyards.

Karma Vista Vineyards

A 460-acre farmstead in Coloma is farmed by sixth-generation farmer Joe Herman. The Hermans have farmed in the region since Jacob Herman arrived from Germany in 1847. Six miles, as the crow flies, from Lake Michigan, the farm benefits from the lake's tempering breezes.

The farmland consists of 150 acres of tart cherry and luscious peach orchards, 50 acres of wine grapes and 90 acres of juice grapes. Like peaches, wine grapes are winter-tender, sensitive fruit that needs to be grown on high ground. Joe's vast acreage provides prime sites for a bounty of agriculture that sometimes changes over the years.

"You can't mess with Mother Nature or economics," says Joe. "Wine grapes are like every other commodity, from apples to oil to cotton. It's supply and demand that drives pricing."

Joe's first plantings of grapes occurred in 1990 for the Welch's Grape Juice Company. The planting of Concords and Niagaras for juice and jelly production eventually led to the planting of wine grapes in the later 1990s. The new plantings inspired Joe and his wife, Sue, to produce wines. They opened a wine-production facility with a tasting room overlooking the beautiful Coloma Valley.

Their winery, Karma Vista Vineyards, is charming, airy and spacious and provides a relaxing interlude along the Lake Michigan Shore Wine Trail. The Hermans produce Pinot Noir, Chardonnay and other varietals, including Sauvignon Blanc, which they initially discovered when it was found accidentally growing in their Merlot vineyard. "We were so surprised to find the grapes growing so well," laughs Joe. "We didn't think Sauvignon Blanc could grow in these soils, but it proved hardy enough." Since then, they've planted additional acreage, producing a wine that is now a customer favorite.

Joe also grows grapes for other vintners, including St. Julian Wine Company. He has been working with Dr. Dave Miller, St. Julian's winemaker since the late 1990s, to plant better clones of Riesling, Pinot Noir, Pinot Grigio and other varietals. In 2009, Joe sold fifty tons of grapes to St. Julian for its wine and juice production. In 2010, the Hermans released their first sparkling wine.

Lemon Creek Winery

Southwest of the Herman farm in Berrien Springs, eight generations of Lemons have tended their 300-acre farm. Since 1855, when Benjamin Lemon started the farm, the family has planted a breadth of fruit, taking full advantage of the region's ideal fruit-growing climate. In 1984, sixth-generation farmer Robert and his wife, Helen, opened a winery along with their sons Bob, Jeff and Tim. Jeff produces the wines, which are 100 percent estate-grown on the rolling, clay loam vineyards consisting of nineteen varietals and 140 acres. One of these varietals is Cabernet Sauvignon; this was the first vineyard of this varietal in Michigan and remains the source for a number of vintners throughout the state. Of note is the winery's Moon Shadow, an ice wine produced from Cabernet Sauvignon grapes left on the vines to freeze naturally. It's the only Cabernet Sauvignon ice wine in the United States.

Winemaker Jeff Lemon is often sought for his farming expertise and lends a hand to other winemakers. Along with wine grapes, sixty acres of other fruits, including raspberries, cherries, apples, peaches, plums and nectarines, are flourishing on the farmland. Today, the Lemon family continues the longtime traditions of their ancestors, tending the land along the lakeshore.

Raftshol Vineyards

About 250 miles north along the east coast of Leelanau Peninsula in Suttons Bay, a third-generation farm has reinvented itself three times. Anders Raftshol established a dairy farm here over a century ago. Cattle were raised until 1930, when Anders's son, Karl, and Karl's wife, Jean, converted the pasture into a cherry orchard that blossomed for forty-five years until the cherry industry began to struggle. In 1975, the cherry trees were pulled from the orchards. Karl passed away in 1977, and Jean worked diligently to keep the family farm for her sons, Warren and Curtis.

Ten years later, in 1985, the brothers planted the farm's first grapevines, consisting solely of European vinifera, a move to which Warren refers as recklessness. The varieties planted were Cabernet Franc, Cabernet Sauvignon, Merlot, Pinot Noir, Chardonnay, Riesling and Gewürztraminer. Incidentally, this was the first commercial planting of red vinifera on the peninsula.

They opened a tasting room in 1999, next to a gray-hued, weathered barn built by their grandfather in 1906. Warren crafted Bordeaux-style wines from their 100 percent estate-grown vinifera. The wine labels were designed with a photo of Jean in her twenties as a tribute to their mother's dedication to saving the family farm.

Chateau de Leelanau Vineyard and Winery

Nearby, two years after the Raftshols planted their vines, Dr. Roberta Kurtz and Joanne Smart bought a hundred-acre cherry and apple farm. In 1989, they replaced just over a quarter of the orchards with grapevines.

"It wasn't long before we decided there were more wine drinkers than cherry pie eaters," says Roberta.

For more than a decade, they sold their grapes to winemakers until deciding to venture into the winemaking business for themselves. They produced their first vintage in 1999 and opened Chateau de Leelanau Vineyard and Winery in Suttons Bay in 2000.

The wines are produced by veteran winemaker John Fletcher, who previously gained a reputation for his wines in British Columbia, Canada, at wine mammoth Vincor International. John is passionate about cool-climate wines and was drawn to Michigan. "The area has special growing conditions that impart wonderful flavors," says John. "No one has the same flavors as northern Michigan."

Although Joanne passed away unexpectedly in 2005, her orchard-to-vineyard project lives on as the source of cool-climate wine production that reflects the flavors of the Leelanau Peninsula farm.

Shady Lane Cellars

Proprietors Joe O'Donnell and Bill Stouten worked with Larry Mawby to launch their dream winery. Twelve acres of grapevines were planted in 1988 on a one-hundred-year-old fruit orchard that formerly bloomed cherry, peach and apple trees. A renovated fieldstone chicken coop housed the tasting room located on Leelanua Peninsula in Suttons Bay.

The winery's first vintages, two *méthode champenoise* sparkling wines, were produced in 1992. The wines, which were released in 1996, are 100 percent Chardonnay Blanc de Blancs and a *brut* produced from Pinot Noir and Chardonnay.

In 2000, they hired Adam Satchwell as winemaker. From the very first vintages, he earned notoriety for the winery, producing wines that garnered many awards. Notable wines are the Pinot Noir, Gewürztraminer and Rieslings, including a sparkling Riesling. Sixty acres are now planted, with Riesling dominating the acreage.

Adam also produces Blue Franc from the Lemberger grape, a varietal used by only a few Michigan vintners thus far. Blue Franc is also known as Blaufrankish and is officially Blauer Limberger.

Today, Shady Lane has fifty-two acres and almost twenty wines.

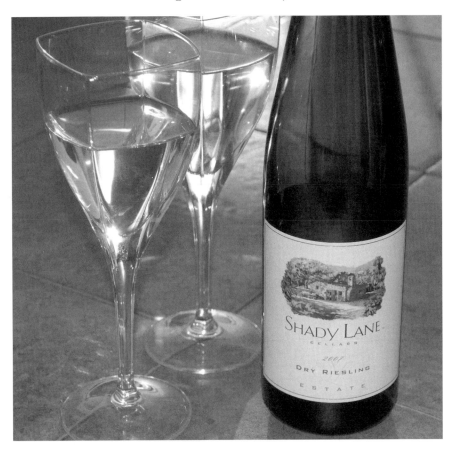

Shady Lane Cellars Dry Riesling.

Peninsula Cellars

Across Grand Traverse Bay on Old Mission Peninsula in Traverse City, the Kroupa family established a farm fifty years before Anders Raftshol. Dave Kroupa, a fourth-generation fruit farmer, tends his family's 250-acre farm that grows cherries, apples and, added in 1991, grapevines. He and his wife, Joan, entered the growing winemaking industry to diversify their fruit farm. They opened Peninsula Cellars tasting room in a nineteenth-century schoolhouse in 1994. The school is the former Maple Grove School, where the peninsula's children were educated from 1885 to 1955.

During the early 2000s, the winery attracts a following under winemaker Bryan Ulbrich for traditional wines, such as Pinot Grigio, Riesling and

Chardonnay, and fun winery monikers, including Homework, Detention and Old School Red. The 2006 Select Riesling garnered Michigan positive press when it represented our state in a 2008 *Time* magazine article, "50 States of Wine." Rated excellent by writer Joel Stein, the Peninsula Cellars wine inspired him to proclaim, "Michigan's Riesling was one of my favorites." British wine authority Tom Stevenson claimed that the winery's Manigold Vineyard Gewürztraminer was the wine he had waited a lifetime to taste—a Gewürz made outside France that tastes like Alsace. Today, the winery continues to garner awards under winemakers John Kroupa and Matt Frollo. John is general manager and the son of Dave and Joan.

The family's cherry farming heritage is honored with White Cherry wine and Hot Rod Cherry, a tribute to Michigan's dynamic auto industry. In 2006, the Kroupas made John a partial owner in the winery. This was the beginning of a succession plan for him to eventually take over complete ownership from his parents.

Farther north on Old Mission Peninsula, two more wineries, Chateau Chantal Winery and Brys Estate Vineyard and Winery, were established on old cherry farmsteads. Though the founders of both wineries were not longtime farmers, they were committed to preserving their breathtaking hillsides for growing fruits.

Chateau Chantal

Chateau Chantal was first established by Bob and Nadine Begin, who had a vision of converting the sixty-five-acre cherry orchard into a world-class wine and travel destination. Incidentally, Bob was a Catholic diocesan priest for twelve years, and Nadine was a Felician sister and teacher for twenty-two years. In 1985, they hired Mark Johnson, who was a winemaker at Chateau Grand Traverse, also on the peninsula. Mark was the third American to graduate from the prestigious wine school of Geisenheim in Germany with a degree in viticulture and enology.

Mark oversaw the planting of wine grape vineyards in the old cherry orchards. The first vines were European vinifera varietals of Chardonnay, Riesling, Pinot Grigio and Gewürztraminer, planted in the spring of 1986. Eventually, 38 acres of the estate were covered with vines. In addition, the winery had 14 acres down the road and tended three other vineyards on the peninsula, for a total of nearly 115 acres of planted agriculture.

Interestingly, Chateau Chantal owns a fifty-five-acre vineyard in the Lujan de Cuyo region of Mendoza, Argentina. Since 2004, Mark has been supervising the vineyard and producing four thousand cases of full-bodied red wine from the Malbec grape. This wine is shipped to the Michigan facility for cellaring and bottling.

In total, the winery produces eighteen thousand cases of wine annually, consisting of more than twenty wine styles, including the winery's popular celebratory sparkling wines, Tonight, a dry blend of Riesling and Chardonnay, and Celebrate, a semidry bubbly made with Chardonnay and a splash of red wine.

Chateau Chantal is located in an awe-inspiring chateau-style building that houses the winery, tasting room, a bed-and-breakfast inn and the Begins' upper-level living residence. The facility opened in July 1993 on top of a hill overlooking the vineyards with views of both East and West Grand Traverse Bays.

In 2009 and 2010, the Begins' daughter, Marie-Chantal Dalese, for whom the winery was named, oversaw a $1.1 million expansion of the tasting room and cellar to meet growing demand for Chateau Chantal wines. Marie-Chantal is director of marketing and works at the winery along with her husband, Paul, who is vineyard manager.

Brys Estate Vineyard and Winery

Another Old Mission Peninsula orchard was revived when Walt and Eileen Brys planted grapevines on an old apple and cherry farm. Morning sunrises reflect on the twenty-five acres of Pinot Noir, Merlot, Cabernet Franc, Riesling, Chardonnay and Pinot Blanc. The Bryses purchased the eighty-acre estate after visiting farms in the wine regions of California, Oregon, New York and Texas.

"We searched for vineyard land and a perfect winery spot. Michigan had all of the things we wanted," says Eileen.

Walt and Eileen carefully renovated an 1890 farmhouse and tractor barn into a home and private guest house and constructed a stunning tasting room, accented with fieldstone and mahogany wood from Honduras. In 2006, Peninsula Township honored them with a preservation award for restoring the estate to a new splendor while retaining the character of the farm.

Cornel Olivier designed the winemaking facility and produced award-winning wines until 2007, when he left to open 2 Lads Winery farther up the peninsula. Coenraad Stassen, also a native of South Africa, took over as winemaker and continues to garner awards for the wines each year. Prior to joining Brys Estate, Coenraad earned a degree at Elsenburg College and learned the art of winemaking in the renowned wine region of Cape Town before attending the international exchange program at Ohio State University and completing his fellowship at Chateau Chantal.

Today, Brys Estate is set up to produce 5,200 cases a year and offers private tastings and winemaker dinners, featuring gourmet entrées paired with its elegant wines.

RIESLINGS ON THE RISE

While cherry orchards were being converted to vineyards, Michigan's established wineries were increasing their production of Riesling. The European vinifera varietal was first planted in Michigan in 1969 on a few acres in Tabor Hill's southwest Michigan vineyard, followed a few years later by significant acreage plantings in northern Michigan at Chateau Grand Traverse in 1976 and 1977. Forty years of growing Riesling proved that the varietal did well in Michigan's diverse climate and soils. And remarkably, it is the fastest-growing white wine in the United States today.

Riesling is a white grape varietal that originated in Germany in the gorgeous Rhine Valley. What's remarkable about Riesling is that the grape expresses the land where it grows and thrives. A Riesling grown in a northwest vineyard dramatically differs from a Riesling grown in a southwest vineyard with the same Lake Michigan influence. Uniquely, a Riesling grown in one vineyard on a peninsula may taste significantly different from a Riesling grown in another vineyard on the same peninsula.

Of our state's seventy-three wineries, most are producing at least one style of Riesling. There are many wineries throughout Michigan that are succeeding in growing and producing world-class Riesling wines.

Stuart Pigott, a British journalist and wine critic working in Germany who often writes about Rieslings, states, "The Michigan Rieslings have been getting better and better the last few years, and in terms of quality, the very best Michigan Rieslings are world-class wines in the medium-bodied dry to off-dry direction.

One of our state's most notable Riesling producers is Chateau Grand Traverse. The O'Keefe family has built their reputation around their high-quality Riesling wines. Their commitment to the varietal is evident in their eighty estate acres and another forty acres under contract. The winery's original 1970s-planted Rieslings are still used in production today. Overall, Michigan has four hundred acres of Riesling; Chateau Grand Traverse's Riesling vineyards grow 20 percent of the total Riesling grapes in the state.

"Riesling is an economically viable grape," explains Eddie O'Keefe III, the elder son of Chateau Grand Traverse founder Ed O'Keefe. "It's conducive to different styles and it's consistent in quality from year to year." Chateau Grand Traverse makes seven different styles of Riesling. Eddie was also a founding member of the International Riesling Foundation, of which he is director. The foundation was established in 2008 to "increase awareness, understanding, and appreciation of Riesling wines produced throughout the world."

One of the foundation's first successes was establishing a global Riesling scale, or taste profile, for labels, indicating the style of Riesling from dry to sweet. The taste profile indicates how the taste of Riesling can vary and appeal to consumers who prefer drier-style wines, as well as to consumers who love sweet wines. As of today, more than one million cases of wine globally feature this new profile on their labels.

Chateau Grand Traverse

At Chateau Grand Traverse, Riesling is the core of the O'Keefes' business and has been since its establishment. The family-owned business has grown from its scrappy, Wild West beginnings to a sophisticated and well-respected powerhouse winery. The O'Keefes are determined to put Michigan on the global map for high-quality, world-class Rieslings and other vinifera wines.

Key to the winery's evolution were years of "shoveling every bit of money" back into the business, as well as fifteen years of focus on developing distribution channels and a costing model for wine production, explains twenty-five-year industry veteran Eddie O'Keefe, who is president of the winery. He readily admits that this isn't the romantic side of the business.

"The winery is a business," says Eddie. "It's not all lit candles, swirling wines and oak barrels. If you don't run the winery like a business, as we say in the industry, a fool and his money are soon parted."

Eddie was only twelve when he began working in the vineyard under the tutelage of his father, Ed. Eddie began managing the day-to-day operations in 1985, upon graduating from Michigan State University.

Operating a winery on Old Mission Peninsula in the 1970s, and even in the present day, was a bit like trying to do business in the Wild West, Eddie says. To fly in experts from California or Europe was cost exorbitant. And there was no factory support or handy equipment technicians, forcing the O'Keefes to adapt and learn how to repair and manage everything themselves.

"You're agriculture, manufacturing, retail, distribution, hospitality, bed-and-breakfast and tour guide. Essentially, you're a jack-of-all-trades who must be financially savvy to survive," he says.

Starting in the late 1990s, Eddie, working with his dad, literally drove distribution for Chateau Grand Traverse wines from the ground up. A warehouse of wine instigated the plan to develop distribution channels. Initially, Eddie loaded up a rented truck and drove the family's wine to different retail outlets. This quickly became too time-consuming, though.

"We had to develop distributor relationships," explains Eddie. "We worked hard, developed a pricing and delivery structure that was consistent and, of course, produced consistently high-quality wines."

The winery also invested in state-of-the-art tanks, pressing and harvesting equipment and, more recently, a bottling line that doubled production capacity in the same amount of time as the old line. With its 20 percent growth in 2009, the winery is on track to produce ninety-five thousand cases in 2010. High-quality wines and distribution are essential to Chateau Grand Traverse's continued growth in Michigan and beyond. The winery has the vision to distribute wines into ten to fifteen states in the future

Chateau Grand Traverse is firmly following Ed's original vision to produce renowned European vinifera wines. Dominating this vision are the plantings of more vineyards. This has been largely overseen, in recent years, by younger brother and vice-president Sean O'Keefe and winemaker Bernd Croissant. Bernd, who has been with the winery since 1993, comes from a family winemaking history tracing back five centuries in Germany.

Sean and Bernd consistently produce top-quality wines. Bernd focuses on making sure the products are consistent year after year. Sean develops eclectic, artistic and high-end specialty wines. A 2009 release that reflects his passion for stylish wines is the Lot 49 Riesling. The wine was made with grapes from a single vineyard site, rather than from multiple vineyard

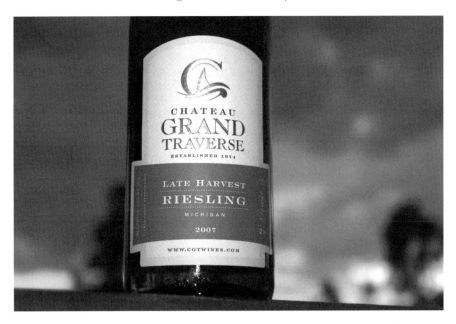

Chateau Grand Traverse Late Harvest Riesling.

locations. Using grapes from a single vineyard enables the winemakers to craft wines that express the character of a specific *terroir*. According to Sean, the result is a wine "with a sense of place that is just more." Sean is also focused on implementing vineyard practices that are as environmentally friendly as feasibly possible. Chateau Grand Traverse is currently producing nine different styles of Riesling, all of which are award winning.

Beyond Riesling, the winery's 120 estate areas of vineyards are laden with European varietals like Chardonnay, Pinot Grigio, Pinot Noir, Gamay Noir, Merlot and Gewürztraminer. Founder Ed O'Keefe is still at the winery every day, generating ideas and working with Eddie on the financial end of the business. Of utmost importance to the O'Keefes is to continue to produce world-class European-style wines that represent the land where they are grown. On a regular basis, the three O'Keefes and Bernd taste and evaluate wines and discuss new concepts to improve wine production.

Like Chateau Grand Traverse, several other Michigan wineries are producing high-quality Rieslings as well, ranging from dry Rieslings to late harvest Rieslings.

ICE WINE: THE INTENSE, NATURAL SWEETNESS OF A COLD HARVEST

Michigan's sloping countryside and dynamic four seasons give winemakers the tools to plant diverse varietals and make wines reflective of our Great Lakes region. A showpiece style of wine made by about one-fourth of our winemakers is the romantic ice wine. Bill Warner of Warner Vineyards has vivid memories of making "frozen wine" in the late 1960s.

"My grandfather and father would wake us up and drop us off in the middle of the night in the vineyards to pick shriveled-up raisins. He'd tell us what rows to pick and that he'd be back in a few hours. We had to hurry so the grapes wouldn't thaw. We kept the juice cold, and a wine full of flavor was made," recalls Bill.

However, it wasn't until 1980 that commercial ice wine was produced on a consistent basis in Michigan. Winemaker Roland Pfleger, heir to a four-hundred-year-old German winery in the Pfalz region, handcrafted the first modern-day ice wine with Riesling at Chateau Grand Traverse. Since then, the winery has produced nine vintages for every year the weather has cooperated.

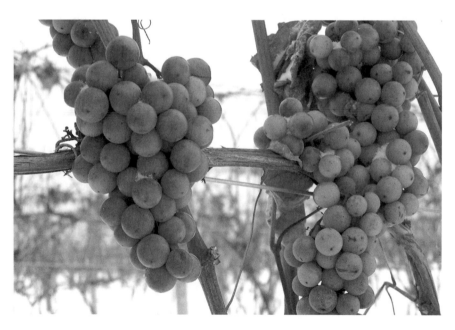

Iced grapes ready for a December harvest at Longview Winery on Leelanau Peninsula.

Ice wine is handcrafted from grapes left on the vines to freeze naturally in cold climates. Michigan's climate is perfectly suited to ice wine production. Consistent temperatures in the mid-teens (seventeen to eighteen degrees Fahrenheit) for a few consecutive days freeze the grapes. The natural freezing solidifies the water in the grape, causing an increased concentration of sugar. The perfectly frozen fruit is carefully handpicked once the grapes are frozen and immediately pressed to retain the high concentration of sugar.

"Ice wine is all about the sugar," explains Bryan Ulbrich, vintner for Left Foot Charley of Traverse City, who produces a traditional-style Vidal Blanc ice wine. "The cool part of ice wine is tasting the concentration from the freezing process. It's the interplay between the rich punch of sugars and that edge of acidity that dances back and forth."

Ice wine is a high risk for the vintner each year. First, the fruit must remain healthy, surviving various climate conditions such as warm and rainy weather that can cause it to rot and blizzard conditions that may cause it to be buried by snow or beaten by sleet. In addition, birds and raccoons are tempted to eat the fresh grapes, so netting is commonly used to protect the fruit from prying claws. If nature doesn't cooperate, vintners may lose their entire harvest for ice wine.

Once grapes are harvested, they are immediately pressed. Only a miniscule amount of liquid is extracted from each grape, thus requiring tons of fruit to squeeze out gallons of juice for ice wine. Once the juice completes the fermentation process, the result is a high-end, flavor-intense dessert wine.

"Ice wine is the ultimate challenge for winemakers," shares Alan Eaker, vintner of Longview Winery on Leelanau Peninsula.

> *Everything must come together. We're dealing with the highly concentrated nectar from grapes, as opposed to the whole grape. This rich environment of sugar and acidity makes fermenting the juice into a finished wine a challenge. These tough Michigan winters are wonderful. Without them, we can't have ice wine. And, what doesn't kill us, makes us feel wonderful.*

Since climate is a key factor in ice wine production, not every wine region can produce a high-quality product. Michigan is one of a short list of ice wine regions. But ice wine is not the only unique product produced in Michigan.

BARRELS AND TANKS TO COPPER STILLS

Fifteen years ago, micro distilleries were not legal in Michigan. Now there are 14, of which at least 5 are on winery properties. Not bad, considering there are roughly 130 to 140 small artisanal distilleries total in the United States. So how did Michigan kick-start its spirit production? Interestingly, it was launched to stimulate the state's fruit industries.

In the early 1990s, Kris Berglund, PhD, university distinguished professor of forestry and chemical engineering at Michigan State University, and Philip Korson II of the Cherry Marketing Institute investigated the possibility of distilling fruits for the production of fruit brandy. The search was instigated by the need to utilize Michigan's often-ample fruit surplus, particularly cherries and apples. The first effort to launch a new agricultural manufacturing industry was deterred by Prohibition-era, anti-distilling laws.

Thanks to a law change in 1996, the opportunity arose again for wineries and breweries to obtain micro distillery licenses. The licenses support the annual production of fruit spirits up to sixty thousand gallons for a nominal licensing fee, whereas before, the fee was $10,000. One caveat, however, is that the winery or brewery must invest in new distilling equipment before a license is issued.

This law change triggered a weeklong research trip to the Black Forest region of Germany, renowned for its spirit *kirsch wasser* (cherry water). The trip was partly funded by the Cherry Marketing Institute and Project GREEEN (Generating Research and Extension to meet Economic and Environmental Needs), Michigan's plant agriculture initiative at Michigan State University.

The research team consisted of Mark Johnson of Chateau Chantal, Kris Berglund and his postdoctorate student, Klaus Weispfenig, and Chas Catherman and Larry Gilbert of St. Julian Wine Company. They toured still manufacturers, brandy producers and research facilities that specialized in fruit brandy production.

Within the week, hand-pounded copper and stainless steel stills were ordered from Christian CARL, Germany's oldest distillery fabricator. The stills were acquired by Michigan State University, Chateau Chantal and St. Julian Wine Company. Vintner Lee Lutes of Black Star Farms and Vintner Rick Moersch of Round Barn Winery quickly acquired stills as well. Experimental brandy production was launched as a natural extension of wine production. Essentially, brandy is distilled wine. Interestingly, the name brandy comes from *brandewijn*, which is Dutch for "burnt wine." The launch of fruit brandy production played an integral role in diversifying key agricultural products while providing an opportunity for Michigan wineries to offer a wider variety of products. A handful of wine producers took the plunge.

Chateau Chantal

One of these wineries was Chateau Chantal of Old Mission Peninsula. The winery produces grape brandy every year and, when ample fruit supply is available, cherry, pear and plum eau de vie. The winery has the capacity to produce up to six thousand gallons of distilled spirits, though its production levels are much lower than capacity. The still, which has been housed in a non-temperature-controlled gazebo, is moving into a winter-friendly facility in 2010, making yearlong production of brandy a more viable option. Nonetheless, the profit to wineries on each bottle of brandy is relatively low, making brandy production more of a passion than a profit-generating venture.

This passion inspired the idea for Entice, a port-style wine made from the juice of an ice wine harvest. Winemaker Mark Johnson arrested the fermentation of the ice wine juice with the addition of grape brandy, resulting in a wine that is about 20 percent residual sugar. He then aged the blend of iced Vidal and Riesling in oak for roughly ten months. According to Mark, "People love the intense flavors of ice wine with the traditional heavier flavors and higher alcohol of a port."

Cherry Cerise is the winery's most renowned distilled product to date. First produced in 2005, Cherry Cerise is made with tart Michigan Montmorency cherries that are fermented before cherry brandy is added to intensify flavors. Cerise Noir is a newer, fermented Pinot Noir that is arrested with the addition of cherry brandy.

St. Julian Winery

The first winery to get a brandy to market under the new law, St. Julian Wine Company of Paw Paw experimented with tart cherries, peaches, raspberries, pears and the pawpaw fruit that grows wild in nearby river valleys in Michigan. Two years after the Christian CARL still arrived, still master Larry Gilbert crafted St. Julian's Williams Christ eau de vie, using locally grown Bartlett pears. The fruit brandy won a gold medal at an Austrian distilled spirits competition.

"Williams Christ is the quintessential eau de vie," says Chas Catherman. "I rank this in the top ten accomplishments in the history of the Michigan wine and fruit spirits industry."

The company is now focused on the continued production of aged grape brandy, recently renamed to A&G as a tribute to vintner David Braganini's two children, Angela and Gene. A nine-year-old brandy was released in early 2010, while another $100,000 worth of brandy is still in the aging process. Under the same micro distilling license, St. Julian produces grape vodka called Grey Heron, which is distilled and filtered five times for a clean, rich-tasting finish.

Black Star Farms

At Black Star Farms in Suttons Bay, the top-selling distilled products are the pear and cherry brandies and dessert wines fortified with brandies.

"The pear brandy is effusive, while the cherry brandy represents our locality," explains winemaker Lee Lutes. It's the winery's eye-catching pear-in-a-bottle brandy that garners the most attention, though.

Preservation of a pear farm that used to supply pears to Gerber for baby food led Black Star Farms to produce the stylish Pear and Its Spirit. Every spring, bottles are carefully placed over the buds sprouting on the Bartlett pear trees. The blossoming pears grow inside the bottles. At harvest time in early September, the branches are very carefully snipped, trapping the pear inside. Bottles are hand-washed, and fifteen to twenty pounds of fruit are distilled to produce a single bottle of pear brandy, which is poured into each bottle. The result is a showpiece for the winery reflective of this growing method that originated in the Alsace region of France hundreds of years ago.

Black Star Farms' brandy production was delayed for two years as the winery-distillery relocated its still from Leelanau Peninsula to a separate still house at the winery's sister winery on Old Mission Peninsula. The new license took two years to obtain, though production is now ramping up, and Lee is targeting one thousand cases a year, possibly more in future years as interest in exploring artisan, regional cuisine grows.

Lee intends to continue handcrafting eau de vie, which he describes as the crème de le crème of spirits. "Good eau de vie plays a role in fine cuisine," says Lee. "Our chef [at the inn] uses the brandy to top salads and produce chutneys, compotes and vinaigrettes. He has served a roast pork loin with

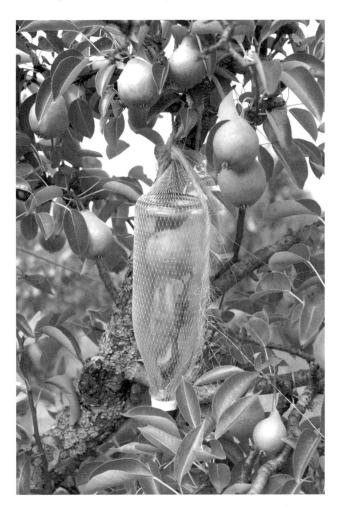

A Bartlett pear budding inside a wine bottle for Black Star Farms' Pear and Its Spirit brandy.

pear chutney with pear brandy over the loin. The aromas were screaming off the plate."

Round Barn Winery

Brandy is also a frequent feature in recipes offered by Round Barn Winery in Baroda. The Moersch family has been producing spirits since the late 1990s, and Sherrie Moersch, a former teacher and a self-taught chef, cooks up artisan dishes using the spirits crafted by her husband, Rick, and son, Matt.

Vintner Rick Moersch, a former high school biology teacher, thoroughly enjoys experimenting. His position as winemaker for Tabor Hill in the 1980s gave him the opportunity to work with a renowned French Champagne producer for several years. It was this experience that ignited an appreciation for looking into the future and allowing wine and spirits to evolve into something more.

Rick jumped at the chance to produce brandies when the new law was passed in 1996. He purchased a still for his winery, and to house his still, he relocated an 1881 round barn from Indiana. Rick strategically selected the round barn to host only good spirits. Rick proclaims, "You won't find any bad spirits lingering here. The devil can't hide if there aren't any corners."

Today, the round barn is a showpiece of the farmstead, and the brandies and dessert wines boast aromatic flavors from apricots, apples, cherries, walnuts, plums, black currants, pears and raspberries. Originally, the winery opened as Heart of the Vineyard in August 1992, though the Moersches changed the name in 2004 to showcase the family's historic round barn.

The Moersches produce a wide selection of wines, brews and distilled spirits. A customer favorite is black currant dessert wine fortified with brandy; this is believed to be the first release in the United States. This wine is modeled after crème de cassis produced in the Burgundy region of France. Another easy-selling customer favorite is grappa, an Italian brandy made from the residue of grapes—skins, stems and seeds—that remains after pressing,

Round Barn Winery has racked up awards and garnered significant media attention for DiVine vodka, made from estate grapes. General manager Chris Moersch, Rick and Sherry's elder son, shares that they are now focused on selling DiVine vodka from their tasting room and a few select retail outlets and growing their customer base more organically than when they first launched DiVine beyond Michigan. "We need to maintain our farmland," says Chris. "We're surrounded by really great fruit, and there are many different ways to use them."

Go Green: Distilling Boosts Michigan's Bioeconomy

MSU now has four stills, ranging from ten to eight hundred liters. The stills reside in Webberville at the Michigan Brewing Company. MSU researchers work closely with wineries, breweries, cider producers and distilleries to research new ideas for growing Michigan's distilled spirit market. The university continues to collaborate with the Cherry Marketing Institute and the Michigan Apple Committee on marketing these agricultural commodities.

MSU is also assisting industries and universities beyond Michigan in developing spirits using diverse agricultural products and is believed to be the only university to have a distilling and commercial license.

Spirit production is a benefit to Michigan's branding as an agritourism destination. The production of spirits utilizes Michigan's vast array of agriculture, from rye to cherries, apples, peaches and plums. Our high-quality, handcrafted spirits are a complement to the award-winning wines and brews produced in the state.

In 2008, the Michigan Economic Development Corporation calculated that Michigan had the potential to generate a $400-million-a-year impact on the economy by manufacturing spirits using the state's agricultural bounty. Spirits generate nearly $1 billion in sales every year, with most of the profits leaving Michigan. The state's wineries would benefit greatly from just a small fraction of this market.

To keep attracting new customers, the innovators are looking at producing more fruit cherry vodkas, grain-based products and products using Michigan's surplus of apples. Fifth-generation farmer Mike Beck of Uncle Johns is releasing the state's first apple vodka in conjunction with Kris Berglund in 2010.

"The texture of vodka is affected by the fruit," says Kris. "We see the biggest growth area in fruit vodkas."

Mike also supplies MSU with apple surplus to aid in the university's experimental research. Round Barn Winery is releasing a new rum in the summer of 2010. Black Star Farms is investigating the production of a new spirit as well.

"Distilleries are another piece of growing Michigan's bioeconomy," states Kris. "We're taking renewable resources and turning them into a high-value, high-quality product."

The Uphill Climb to Reach Consumers

Generally, Americans are not familiar with the taste of fruit brandies and, in particular, eau de vie, a colorless fruit brandy that is more aptly described as an orchard in a bottle for its explosive, aromatic flavor derived from fifteen to twenty pounds of premium fruit per bottle. Eighty proof eau de vie is for sipping as a *digestif* at the end of a meal to clear the palate and aid digestion. In Europe, eau de vie is traditionally enjoyed to cap off meals.

In the past, educating consumers about brandies has been prohibitive. Offering samples of the labor-intensive, high-quality brandy is costly. And for the first ten years of brandy production, wineries were unable to charge for tastings of these spirits, and spirits can only be sold from the location where the still resides. Wineries with multiple tasting rooms cannot sell their brandies at remote locations without investing in additional stills and personnel to produce spirits at these locations.

Perhaps the biggest challenge is that Michigan's government acts as a wholesaler for distilled spirits. To reach customers beyond the tasting room, wineries (and breweries) must produce enough brandy to meet a minimum sales quota to be able to sell through the government's distribution channels to retailers and restaurants. Since our wineries see brandy production as a complement to wine production and fruit processing, high production volumes are not easily reached. If any Michigan brandy, or spirit, actually makes it to store shelves, it is competing with more familiar spirits, like Jim Beam bourbon or Smirnoff vodka. Without the opportunity to educate consumers about our unique fruit spirits, the expense to reach them via store placement is generally not worth the extra production effort. On top of this, spirits are heavily taxed.

These challenges led Kris Berglund of MSU, now renowned for his expertise in micro distilling in the United States, to initiate a new law in 2008. Significant support from state representative Barb Byrum aided in the implementation of Act 218 of the 2008 Public Acts, which allows producers to make any type of distilled alcohol under one nominal license fee and enables producers to sell a glass of distilled spirits for a fee in the tasting rooms. This is especially helpful for educating customers about fruit spirits.

Additionally, the new law lifts limitations on what is used to produce distilled spirits. Grain-based spirits, fruit vodkas, rums and other spirits can now be produced under a single micro-distilling license. Once again, this enables wineries to diversify beyond wine and brandy and use every aspect of the fruit to develop unique products that express Michigan's agricultural bounty. The passing of Act 218 signifies the collaboration of many key organizations, including the university, producers and lawmakers.

In 2009, a bill was introduced to amend the 2008 distilling law to enable wineries to sell their spirits from all tasting room locations without the need for a still and production at each location. Unfortunately for the wineries, this amendment was not passed.

Twelve years of challenges have slowed down spirit production by wineries, though not the spirits of our winemakers who persevere and passionately believe that our agriculture is our state's greatest asset. While challenges are being faced within the spirits industry, the state's vintners and researchers are continuing to test new grapevines in search of more varietals that will flourish in the state's climate and soils. At the same time, winemakers are producing wines from varietals that are already flourishing and have been proven to make great wine.

1990s: WINERIES ON THE RISE

A farmer or gardener, on a grand or small scale, knows the excitement of planting something for the first time. Patiently, they wait for their investment

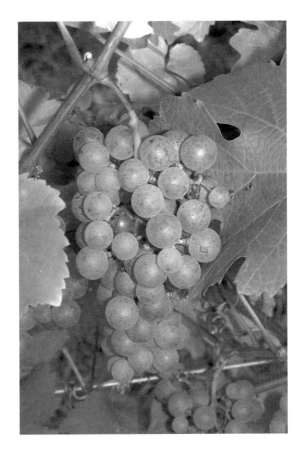

Diverse wine grape varietals flourish in Michigan.

to grow, bud and, hopefully, produce robust juicy fruit year after year. Winemakers share this intrigue, and in many cases, they play the role of scientist, experimenting with traditional and lesser-known grape varietals in varied soils. They passionately and patiently research, plant and test before crafting and tasting to achieve that "Ah-ha!" moment.

In Michigan, there are currently more than fifty grape varietals growing in our soils, with ten varietals earning the most acreage. Along with Riesling, the largest concentration of grapevines includes Chardonnay, Pinot Grigio/Pinot Gris, Cabernet Franc, Gewürztraminer, Merlot, Pinot Noir and three hybrids—Vignoles, Vidal Blanc and Seyval Blanc. However, it's not just these wines that you'll find in the tasting rooms. Several Michigan wineries are producing quality wines from less well-known varietals. Michigan's mounting reputation for growing grapes and producing wines dramatically increased the production of one of Michigan's 1970s-established wineries and inspired thirteen wineries to open their doors in the 1990s.

Leelanau Wine Cellars

After its establishment in the mid-1970s, Leelanau Wine Cellars continued to implement innovative changes in planting, production and marketing to keep up with its steady increase in sales each year. Vintner Mike Jacobson added Chardonnay, Riesling, Pinot Noir, Merlot, Cabernet Franc, Vignoles and Baco Noir based on results from a one-and-a-half-acre test vineyard consisting of thirty varietals that he planted in 1984 in collaboration with Michigan State University. Some of the test varietals were Chardonnay, Sauvignon Blanc, Pinot Noir, Cabernet Franc, Merlot, Cabernet Sauvignon, Lemburger, Pinot Gris and Muscat.

Production, which peaked in the early years at fifteen thousand cases of wine a year, experienced a dramatic drop in 1985 and caused Mike to further invest in the winery through the 1990s to grow the business. Chuck Kalchik, Mike's partner in the winery, decided he wanted to focus solely on farming. Mike bought his interest in the company, becoming sole owner of the winery, and began to reorganize the business.

The wine labels were redesigned for a fresh, new look and brand, and a new line of blended wines with proprietary names was developed. Mike and his winemaker, Bill Skolnik, determined that some wines, even though they were of good quality, were too challenging to sell if consumers couldn't connect with the unfamiliar varietal names. The new wines, which Bill produced using the less familiar French-American hybrid grape varietals, featured a seasonal line including Spring Splendor, Summer Sunset, Autumn Harvest and Winter White. Notably, one of the seasonal wines, Winter White, although not produced with Michigan grapes, was the state's top-selling wine in 2009. As a side note, the seasonal wines were originally produced with all Michigan fruit, though they were later subsidized as demand outgrew the winery's ability to source locally.

In 1999, Cabernet Sauvignon and Pinot Gris were added to the vineyard behind its production facility in Omena, and the 1984 test vineyard was replaced with Merlot. Throughout the first decade of the 2000s, the Jacobsons updated production equipment to handle further growth to keep up with demand.

In 2001, longtime employee Shawn Walters took over the winemaking, while he continued to be involved in improving vineyard practices. Shawn had been with the winery since 1993, though he departed for a two-year stint to assist winemaker Lee Lutes of Black Star Farms with the opening of the new Suttons Bay winery. For Leelanau Wine Cellars, he helped drive annual production increases with the planting and expansion of vineyards.

Shawn maintained a focus on diversifying and experimenting with grape varietals and won several awards for the winery. Notably, the 2005 Merlot made the list of the "30 Best American Merlots" with an eighty-eight rating in the October issue of *Wine & Spirits Magazine*.

In 2007, Nichole Birdsall, a native of Healdsburg, California, located in the heart of Sonoma Wine Country, took over as winemaker when Shawn left to start a wine consulting firm. Nichole earned an enology degree from California State University–Fresno before working for Korbel Champagne Cellars and as an organic winemaker at Bonterra Vineyards, a division of Fetzer Vineyards. She quickly adapted to Michigan grape growing and wine production and is implementing new soil nutrient practices to the vineyards. She is working closely with Dr. Marcel Lenz, who manages the vineyards. Together, they are focused on growing and producing quality wine. Several of Nichole's products have won wide acclaim and medals, adding to the long list of awards achieved by the winery throughout its history.

Today, Leelanau Wine Cellars has eighty-five acres of grapevines planted in three vineyards. Nichole is expanding vineyards to include additional plantings of Pinot Grigio, Riesling and French-American hybrids to keep up with growing demand for the production of more than thirty varieties of wine.

Jacobson's son, Bob, is now president of Leelanau Wine Cellars and oversees all operations of the business. Upon graduating from college and joining the winery on a full-time basis, Bob was instrumental in increasing distribution of his family's wines. He has led the winery to a production of more than 120,000 cases of wine, with distribution throughout the Great Lakes region, making it the state's largest winery in sales in 2009.

While Leelanau Wine Cellars was ramping up its wine production to keep up with demand, several more wineries opened in the state.

Bel Lago Winery

Dr. Charlie Edson, who holds a PhD in horticulture, first planted a test vineyard in 1987 to experiment with varietals to determine their ability to withstand Michigan's cool climate. Today, his thirty-acre vineyard sits high atop a hill in Cedar overlooking Lake Leelanau. He opened a tasting room in 1999, naming it Bel Lago Vineyard and Winery; *bel lago* translates to "beautiful lake." He produces eighteen wines using grapes from the top ten varietals in Michigan, as well as some less common varietals. He crafts the enigmatic grape Auxerrois (oh-zher-WAH) with fruit tones prevalent in the dry white wine made from grapes originally of the Alsace region of France. In 2010, the Auxerrois won the Chairman's Award, unanimous gold, at Riverside International Wine Competition in California.

Bel Lago also stands out for Tempesta, a blend with Cabernet Franc at the forefront of the big, bold wine aged in American oak. Bel Lago is also part of the state's sparkling wine industry with two bubblies. Incidentally, Charlie's Tempesta was rated a "world-class red," and his *Brut* Sparkling Wine as "one of Michigan's best," by Tom Stevenson, author of *The Sotheby's Wine Encyclopedia* book series.

Bowers Harbor Vineyards

Bowers Harbor Vineyards was the second winery to open on Old Mission Peninsula, joining Chateau Grand Traverse, the sole winery on the peninsula for fifteen years. The Stegenga family purchased a forty-three-acre estate in 1985 and ventured into winemaking five years later. In 1992, a stable for quarter horses was converted to a cozy tasting room opening onto a patio that encourages a leisurely stay overlooking Bowers Harbor.

Vintners Spencer Stegenga and his mother, Linda, are passionate for producing Pinot Grigio and Riesling that reflect good-quality fruit from individual vineyards. The winery produces single-vineyard Rieslings, meaning that all the grapes are pulled from one vineyard to create a wine. This is significant because Riesling is very *terroir* specific, meaning that a Riesling from one vineyard may taste significantly different from a Riesling from another vineyard, even one nearby. While Riesling is a major focus, Pinot Grigio is their flagship wine. The winery also crafts a sparkling wine, Blanc de Blanc, from Chardonnay and Pinot Grigio.

Willow Vineyard

John and Jo Crampton of Willow Vineyards in Suttons Bay are focused on producing four wines using three grape varietals, all of which are estate-grown—Pinot Noir, Pinot Gris and Chardonnay. The fourth wine is Baci Rosé, which they produce from Pinot Noir.

The winery was established after an unexpected stumble across an old, fallen-down sign on the beautiful hillside overlooking West Grand Traverse Bay. After they eventually built a home on the site, the Cramptons were inspired to become farmers by the rich growing conditions of their land. John and Jo claim that it was an evening of drinking wine that prompted them to plant vineyards and become winemakers. The name of their winery is in honor of an old willow tree that was located at the end of their drive until it was struck by lightning and split in two.

Wyncroft

In southwest Michigan, Jim Lester and his wife, Rae Lee, who passed away in 2009, opened Wyncroft Winery in 1998, a winery that operates in the style of a tiny French *garagiste* winery (a group of innovative winemakers in the Bordeaux region producing *vins du garage*, or "garage wine"). Essentially, Wyncroft does not have a tasting room; samples of the high-end, limited release wines are provided through private tastings and are sold by the case. The wines are also available in a select group of fine restaurants.

The goal when opening the winery was to craft world-class wines that reflect the Lake Michigan shore microclimate. The wines are grown in the longer growing season and in the mineral-rich soils within ten miles of the Lake Michigan shoreline. Jim focuses solely on crafting artisanal European-style wines expressing individual vineyards. From the start, his marketing strategically positioned the winery as higher end. Wyncroft produces Pinot Noir, Chardonnay, Riesling and their flagship wine, Shou (the Chinese symbol for longevity). Shou wine is a blend of Cabernet Sauvignon, Merlot and Cabernet Franc in the style of the wines of Pauillac and Margaux.

Chateau Fontaine Vineyards and Winery

Dan and Lucie Matthies of Chateau Fontaine in Lake Leelanau are also producing Auxerrois, under the brand Woodland White. The Matthieses began wine grape plantings in 1989 on a former cow pasture and potato farm, where their personal residence is situated. They initially supplied grapes to nearby Good Harbor Vineyards, eventually deciding to produce wines on their own.

"We were already interested in wines and already had these beautiful vineyards," Lucie reflects regarding their decision. They produced their first commercial vintage in 1999 and opened a tasting room at the bottom of their vineyard hill in 2000. The winery is located at roughly nine hundred feet on the French Road plane on Leelanau Peninsula in an area that has vineyards among the highest in Michigan, at one thousand to thirteen hundred feet above sea level.

Today, the winery has three vineyards totaling twenty-two acres of Chardonnay, Pinot Gris, Gewürztraminer, Riesling, Pinot Noir, Merlot and small amounts of a few others grape varieties.

Jomagrha Vineyards and Winery

Jomagrha's winemaker and proprietor, John Sanford, produces a selection of limited-quantity table wines, many of which are named for the area. The winery, which opened in 1999, was named using the first two letters of John's family members: John, Mary, Graham and Harry. Before starting his winery, John planted twenty-three varietals in a test lot to determine which were best suited for his farm, located one mile east of the shores of Lake Michigan. Today, the farm grows seven acres of grapevines.

Nicholas Black River Vineyard and Winery

Nicholas Koklanaris arrived in the United States from Ikaria, Greece, in 1955. After retiring, he researched wine grapes to find hearty varietals that could withstand the cold northern climate. In 1992, he planted grapevines along the Black River in Cheboygan for hobby winemaking to carry on the traditions of his Greek grandfather. The vines were planted by digging holes with an army shovel every six inches and mixing black dirt and sand for optimum growth. He personally nurtured and tended to each vine as they matured.

In 1999, he opened Nicholas Black River Vineyard and Winery with a tasting room in Cheboygan, followed in 2004 with a second tasting room in Mackinaw City. The tasting room in Cheboygan features beautiful hand-painted wall murals that depict the family's history, starting in Ikaria and arriving in America.

After Nicholas passed away, he left the winery to his nieces, Maria and Alea Melacrinos, who moved to Michigan from Greece. Maria worked as an apprentice to her uncle before his passing. Today, the sisters' father, Dimitrios Melacrinos, is the winemaker. A selection of thirteen wines is produced, one of which is called Nick's Dry Red in honor of Nicholas.

Peterson and Sons Winery

Vintner Duane Peterson opened his winery in 1983 with the focus to produce wines without any chemicals or preservatives. Initially, his winery operated from the basement of his home, though he moved it into the garage a year later as business grew. By 1988, his business justified a new wine production facility located next to his home.

Duane's wine list varies, though the list always features fruit wines, such as black raspberry, cherry and wild elderberry, and at least one red or white grape varietal, such as Chambourcin, Niagara or Chardonel. His wines are favored for their light taste and all-natural ingredients, which he markets as the "no headache wines."

Today, he serves customers from the winery tasting room tucked in the countryside of Kalamazoo, though his basement tasting room is still available for more intimate tastings.

Tartan Hill Winery

Oceana County is situated along Lake Michigan, about halfway from the tip of Michigan's lower mitten to the bottom. In 1985, Tartan Hill Winery, the county's first and only winery, was opened by Bob and Carol Cameron.

Since then, the winery has changed ownership to Paul and Beverly Goralski, who operate the wine production business along with their son, Greg, and daughter-in-law, Renae. The winery, which was named in honor of the founding owners' Scottish heritage, sits on top of a beautiful vista on a homestead in New Era within a few miles of the lakeshore. The vineyard catches the lake breezes and grows a variety of grapes, including Cayuga, Seyval Blanc, Marechal Foch and Cabernet Franc.

Greg handcrafts wines that are 100 percent estate-grown and bottled, offering fifteen wines on the tasting list. In 2009, the winery released a blend of Traminette and Gewürztraminer.

AGRICULTURAL DIVERSITY: 2000 AND BEYOND

The industry experienced many changes from the 1980s through the late 1990s. Increased funding for wine grape research and the establishment of four American Viticultural Areas strengthened Michigan's wine industry foundation. Sparkling wine and ice wine added pizzazz to the offerings of many wineries. The distilling movement ultimately opened the doors for wineries to diversify agricultural offerings even further with fruit brandies, eaux de vie and vodkas. Michigan winemakers are passionate about experimenting and releasing hard apple and pear ciders (Perry) and honey meads made with cherries and blueberries and other fruits. Michigan's biodiverse agriculture gives producers ample fresh ingredients to make these products.

Michigan's wine industry was booming. Almost fifty wineries opened by the early 2000s. Today, a total of seventy-three wineries are in operation, an increase of almost 500 percent since the Michigan Grape and Wine Industry Council started in 1985. The wine industry is in a position to strengthen Michigan's image as a manufacturing machine of agricultural bounty. Unfortunately, the industry continues to wrestle with state regulations that prohibit its growth.

THE MICHIGAN SHIPPING ISSUE

In 2003, Eleanor and Ray Heald, wine writers since 1978, led the charge to strike down an anti-commerce law, a clause of the Twenty-first

Amendment repealing Prohibition in 1933. The Healds sued the State of Michigan in regard to discriminatory and anticompetitive direct shipping laws that adversely affected fair trade into Michigan. As wine writers, they often ordered wines from around the world. Michigan's antiquated laws prohibited the direct shipment of wine from other states to consumers living in Michigan. On August 28, 2003, the Healds prevailed in *Heald v. Engler* in the U.S. Sixth Circuit Court of Appeals. However, the State of Michigan responded by defending its regulations and appealed the decision to the U.S. Supreme Court as *Granholm v. Heald*.

The *Granholm v. Heald* defense by the State of Michigan prompted Michigan's vintners to organize an initiative to protect individual winery interests and the rights of the wineries to sell direct to their customers. At the same time, a consumer initiative called WineCam was launched to organize consumers to fight for their rights. On May 16, 2005, the U.S. Supreme Court decided in favor of the Healds, stating that Michigan's direct shipping laws were, indeed, unconstitutional. This initiative and the persistence of the Healds opened new market opportunities for the state's wineries.

PRODUCTION ON THE RISE

The early 1980s witnessed an all-time low production in Michigan, with 250,000 cases of wine annually. This was a 75 percent drop from the annual 1,000,000 cases of wine once produced during the early 1960s. Fortunately for the state's wine industry, production is once again on the rise, reaching 350,000 cases by 2006 and 500,000 cases by 2009. The industry is taking the future of the Michigan wine industry very seriously and has set a target to grow ten thousand acres of wine grapes and produce 3,000,000 cases of wine by 2024. Today, a solid foundation is in place for the Michigan wine industry to succeed in achieving its objectives.

Our state's climate is ideal for growing diverse wine grapes and a bounty of other agriculture. Michigan's vineyards, situated between the forty-first and forty-seventh parallels with a plethora along the forty-fifth parallel, are producing European vinifera and French-American hybrid grapes and, ultimately, world-class wines. Our winemakers are skilled and experimental, creating stylish wines, fruit brandies and other distilled products, meads and more to strengthen Michigan's brand as a manufacturer of top-quality agricultural beverages. The vineyards are mature, and the wines are garnering national and worldwide attention. More than one hundred tasting rooms are open in wine country to offer diverse experiences in our vineyards and along our wide-open farmland. Michigan wine country is a showcase of passionate winemaking, agriculture, natural resources and Great Lakes.

MICHIGAN

Destination for World-Class Wine and Food Experiences

Michigan winemakers have created unique experiences to introduce their wines in a friendly tasting environment for 150 years. This tradition goes back centuries to the Old World. Wine has always been approachable and inviting. It represents the people who craft it, the vineyard that grows it, the tasting room where it is served and the region it promotes.

Imagine your first visit to a Michigan tasting room in 1870, overlooking Lake Erie as the sun rises above and reflects off the significant Great Lake that cascades down Niagara Falls to the east. Winemakers and business partners Joseph Sterling, William Noble, Caleb Ives and Samual Williams offer a tour of their uniquely constructed Pointe Aux Peaux Wine Company in Monroe. While visiting the tasting room, they invite you down into the sixty-degree cool wine cellar and encourage you to stay while they press grapes or, possibly, sample aged wine direct from a barrel.

Now imagine the excitement of a new highway opening that makes traveling from the bustling cities along the Detroit River to southwest vineyards a breeze. It is 1959, and St. Julian opens its tasting room to the influx of travelers blazing their way to the lakeshore on the weekends. I-94 is now open, and the exit into Paw Paw makes a visit to the tasting room and tour of the production facility part of a weekend travel adventure.

A 1999 adventure finds you jostling along a two-track dirt road on a wagon through 160 acres of grapevines at Fenn Valley Vineyards in Fennville. Vintner Doug Welsch impresses you with his adept skill at unpretentious wine education. The wagon stops amid the vines, and you savor the glorious 360-degree autumn views while tasting wine and enjoying a succulent ready-for-harvest grape plucked from the fruit-filled vines.

EXPERIENCING THE WINES…THE WINE EXPERIENCES

Today, seventy-three wineries and more than one hundred tasting rooms offer an array of wines and experiences. Summer wine and food festivals rock the coasts and attract thousands of visitors. The Leland Wine Fest, on Leland Harbor and within view of Lake Michigan and the Manitou Islands, is a twenty-five-year tradition launched by the late Bruce Simpson of Good Harbor Vineyards. The festival features regional wines, foods and music of northern Michigan. In southwest Michigan, the Lake Michigan Shore Wine Festival's annual Toast the Coast beach bash at Weko Beach in Bridgman features regional wines, foods and live music along the shores of Lake Michigan. One of the state's newer coast festivals is East Tawas Uncork'd and Untap'd, featuring statewide wineries, brews, regional foods, live music and grape stomping along Tawas Bay of Lake Huron.

Away from the breezes of the Great Lakes, discover the Ella Sharp Art and Wine Festival in Jackson, featuring local artwork, wineries of the nearby Pioneer Wine Trail, foods and live music. This festival is on the grounds of the rolling, 562-acre Ella W. Sharp Park, surrounded by hundreds of inland lakes and along the southwest branch of the Grand River.

Michigan Wine Trails

Traveling along one of Michigan's wine trails makes you feel as if you're in a painting. Stately, heritage red barns provide the backdrop to luscious fruit orchards gracing rolling hillsides. White and pink-hued blossoms and plump, juicy fruits brilliantly color the landscapes. Grapevines stretching along vineyard trellises hang like green and autumn-hued scarecrows with dangling, juicy, dark purple and chartreuse grapes.

The essence of our region is captured while traveling organized wine trails in Michigan. The trails consist of neighboring wineries, some within a farmyard's stretch of one another while others may be several miles apart. Four trails exist today, though a fifth wine trail is being considered in Michigan's Upper Peninsula. Touring a wine trail adds regional flair to your day trip, weekend getaway or weeklong adventure. Handy brochures featuring all wineries of the trail may also showcase dining, shopping and recreational experiences along the trail.

The Lake Michigan Shore Wine Trail is located along the southwest Michigan shoreline from the southern border of Michigan to Saugatuck and east to Paw Paw, some of which is along the historic Red Arrow Highway. Fifteen wineries inhabit this trail, including the state's oldest: St. Julian Wine Company and Warner Vineyards.

Our largest trail is on northern Michigan's Leelanau Peninsula, known as the "pinky finger" of Michigan. Be sure to plan more than a day to visit the eighteen wineries nestled along the regionally famous M-22 peninsula drive offering views of Lake Michigan, Lake Leelanau and breathtaking Sleeping Bear Dunes National Lakeshore.

Across the bay, the Wineries of Old Mission Peninsula (WOMP) is the most condensed trail, with seven wineries located along the narrow, seven-mile stretch of farmland that juts into Lake Michigan and is dotted with fruit orchards. Stunning panoramic views of West and Grand Traverse Bay provide a tranquil backdrop to your tour.

In southeast Michigan, discover the Pioneer Wine Trail, consisting of five wineries located throughout the countryside of the Irish Hills region, in historic downtown Tecumseh and along fertile farmland of the Jackson and Grass Lake corridor.

Michigan wine trails are within easy reach, offering day trips and overnight and weekend escapes.

Beyond the Trails

Wineries are located across the state, and wineries are popping up all over on multigenerational farms and in regions that are growing modern-day wine grape vineyards.

Adam Kolodziejski of Rose Valley Winery in Rose City made his first batch of wine from wild grapes found along the Tobacco River. As a biology major at Central Michigan University in 1968, Adam picked the grapes, threw some yeast on them and drank the juice. More than forty years later, he presents fine tuned, artisan wines made with Chambourcin, Chancellor, Vidal, Riesling, Baco Noir and Muscat in his impressive twenty-five-hundred-square-foot winemaking facility in Rose City. The high elevation of the surrounding Ogemaw Hills gives him plenty of airflow for his vineyard to grow on nearby farmland. Along with familiar grape varietals, he is keen on growing cold-hardy grapes, including native-to-Michigan Edelweiss, St. Pippen and Frontenac.

Above the big mitt of the Lower Peninsula lies the vast open recreational paradise of Michigan's Upper Peninsula. Threefold Vine and Garden Bay Winery are on the beautiful Garden Peninsula. Threefold Vine has planted thirty different cold-hardy wine grape varietals in its vineyard. The first winery to open in the Upper Peninsula was Mackinaw Trail Winery of Manistique.

"Tourists arrive from all over, including Minnesota, Wisconsin and Illinois," says Ralph Stabile, vintner of Mackinaw Trail Winery. "We are already at seven thousand cases of wine a year." Ralph works with his son, Dustin, to produce wines, primarily vinifera varietals and fruit wines. They initially planned to grow grapes on the Garden Peninsula, though they are now buying grapes from southwest and northwest Michigan, strawberries and cherries from the Traverse City region and blueberries and cranberries from South Haven. A Mackinaw City tasting room is in a prime location for tourists traveling to this historic region, while a new tasting room location in Petoskey's historic Gaslight District is attracting a local following and the summer cottage crowd. "Michigan-grown is our number one selling point," says Ralph.

Another unique destination is Douglas Valley Organic Vineyard Community in Manistee, with rolling hills that rise as high as nine hundred feet above sea level. Fruit grower and real estate developer Cliff Boom acquired a 1900s-era fruit farm in 2005. The USDA certified organic farm, organic since 1990, is now home to a seasonal farm market amid eight thousand vines of Pinot Grigio and Pinot Noir. The tasting room is a century-old bunkhouse for rail passengers on the former Manistee & North Eastern Railroad. The development offers farm lots large enough for home dwellings and garden-vineyard plots.

Michigan wineries and tasting rooms can be found almost anywhere, such as along a wine trail, in urban settings, among quaint villages and amid preserved farmland. Remarkably, the state's wineries attract more than 800,000 visitors a year, many of whom are enjoying the unique experiences offered across the state.

Michigan

The Michigan Wine Experience

Very often, memorable experiences while sampling wines connect you to the wine itself. You will find myriad experiences to enjoy during each of Michigan's four seasons. A fall-to-spring experience at Round Barn Winery in Buchanan offers the state's only hands-on winemaking class, encompassing the harvest and bottling of wine production.

"We're surrounded by good fruit. We use our natural resources in so many different ways. People want to connect with the land; they want to get out of the city, do a day trip and spend time on the farm and enjoy the natural beauty of our lakeshore. Agritourism is a huge part of Michigan's future," explains Chris Moersch of Round Barn Winery.

Don Coe, managing partner of Black Star Farms of Suttons Bay agrees:

> *Michigan wineries are all about agritourism. The world does not need another winery. Travelers, however, are always seeking out new experiences, and the opportunity to link their interest in wine to a place, a winemaker or a personal discovery is what makes Michigan wines.*

An overnight stay at the luxurious Inn at Black Star Farms may entail a delicious gourmet dinner, a wine sampling and tour in the tasting room and artisan, wood fire–roasted pizza topped with farm-grown ingredients.

So what is agritourism? Seemingly, it's a new trend, though in reality, it's an Old World tradition of connecting visitors to the land and the people who farm it. Walking farm tours and harvesting seasonal fruits and vegetables at the peak of freshness offers a glimpse of life before modernization and refrigeration. In the case of regional wineries, agritourism involves interacting with the winemaker, touring the vineyards and facilities and sampling the wines.

"Agricultural tourism operations, like wineries, are increasingly important to the future of Michigan agriculture and the state economy," says Don Koivisto, director of the Michigan Department of Agriculture.

> *Agriculture and tourism, the state's second and third leading industries, support economic stability and development, strengthen Michigan's family farms, improve the quality of life for our citizens in both rural and urban areas, and preserve the state's rich and diverse farmland and agricultural heritage.*

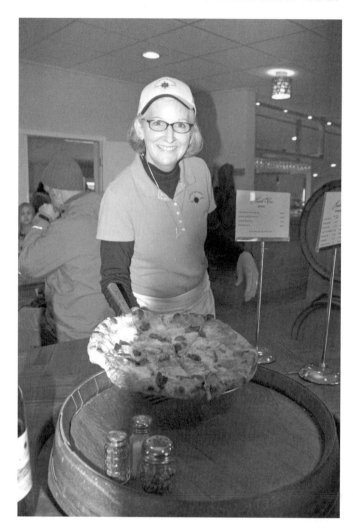

Artisan wood-fire pizza topped with farm-fresh ingredients at Black Star Farms in Suttons Bay.

Agritourism is a fully engaging experience. Take, for instance, Chateau Chantal on Old Mission Peninsula. Certified culinary professional Nancy Krcek Allen teaches hands-on techniques for infusing ingredients into traditional and contemporary-inspired cuisine. The cooking classes are recognized among the best "Gourmet Getaways" in Joe David's book *Gourmet Getaways: 50 Top Spots to Cook and Learn*. He describes the destination as "an American version of a modern Loire Valley chateau; a retreat for gourmets who seek a food and wine holiday."

Dinners hosted by winemakers are another fun venue for experiencing regional foods and wines. Spencer Stegenga, vintner of Bowers Harbor

Vineyards of Old Mission Peninsula in Traverse City, teams with neighboring Boathouse Restaurant to offer two additional experiences: Dining in the Vines and Dining on the Fly. Executive chef Eric Nittolo cooks fresh, regional, gourmet fare in the Bowers Harbor vineyards alongside the Boardman River. The courses are paired perfectly with Spencer's wines for a truly magnificent experience. You'll simply relax while savoring a five-course feast blending contemporary and classic French-style cuisine. Spencer and Eric regale you with stories as you casually dine at a white-linen table nestled between vineyard rows. The second experience entails an entomology lesson, pulling on waders and casting a fly in one of Michigan's legendary Blue Ribbon trout streams. Under the tutelage of fly-fishing guide David McCool, try your luck at catching your own dinner. Regardless of your fly-fishing skill, you're guaranteed a five-course feast artfully prepared by Eric and enjoyed riverside under a white tent speckled with dancing candlelight.

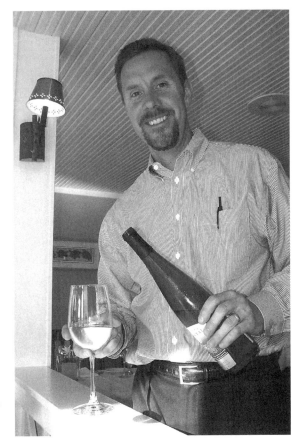

Owner Doug Kosch of Old Mission Peninsula's Boathouse Restaurant invites you to enjoy a glass of Michigan wine.

"We love showcasing our wines on our farm and along the water," says Spencer. "We like creating value-added experiences for people to learn about our wines."

Spencer is also teaming with Stafford's Weathervane Restaurant in Charlevoix overlooking the Pine River Channel. The historic restaurant is a former gristmill, converted into a destination for fine dining by renowned architect Earl Young. Spencer teamed with Stafford's to present fun dining experiences along the channel that connects Round Lake and Lake Michigan. Bowers Harbor Vineyards wines are perfectly paired with featured entrées, such as Michigan potato-crusted whitefish and roasted duck and Michigan asparagus tartlet.

The trend for wine and food experiences is a valuable niche in the Michigan tourism industry. A prime example of meshing tourism and agriculture is the Traverse City National Cherry Festival, the region's eighty-four-year-old flagship event. The eight-day festival is one of the state's largest and greatly impacts the local region, with $26 million and 450 full-time jobs. Wine-related events are among the two hundred activities that attract more than 500,000 people to the region each year.

Agriculture and tourism drive an enormous portion of the state's economy. Remarkably, Michigan agriculture is currently a $71.3 billion industry, and the Great Lake State is the second most agriculturally diverse state in the country, after California.

Multigenerational Farms

Michigan's diversity reflects the passion of multigenerational farmers to maintain and preserve farmland for future generations. Along with the farming families highlighted in earlier chapters, including the Lemons of Lemon Creek Winery and the Kroupas of Peninsula Cellars, there are a handful of other families that are preserving their heritage farmlands with creative, hands-on activities on working farms.

Fox Barn Winery is operated by a fifth-generation farm family. They began offering wines in 2009, including pear and cherry wine. They've integrated a winery into their farm market, where they sell seasonal fruits and vegetables inside an eighty-year-old barn they've coined an "agricultural marketplace." Fox Barn is situated in Shelby in Oceana County, near the Silver Lake Sand Dunes.

Robinette's Apple Haus and Winery of Grand Rapids and Uncle John's Cider Mill and Fruit House Winery of St. Johns are two destinations that provide a variety of activities for all ages; U-pick fruits, wagon rides, wine and hard apple cider tasting are just a few. The Robinette family will celebrate their centennial year of farming in 2011, and similar to the fifth-generation Beck family of Uncle John's, they continue to churn out donuts, ciders and exemplary hospitality.

Rooms with a View

Breathtaking 360-degree views solidify Michigan as a traveler's paradise. A handful of wineries provide jaw-dropping views from within their tasting rooms that look out onto the Great Lakes, flourishing vineyards and rolling farmland. Find your way to these wineries on a wet, rainy day or too-hot afternoon, or whenever you simply want to relax, and savor the wine and soak in the sights.

Along the Lake Michigan Shore Wine Trail, Coloma farmland billows out in all directions. Karma Vista, to the north of highway I-94, offers a view of Coloma Valley from atop its vineyard vista. To the south of I-94, Contessa Wine Cellars pours European-influenced wines in crystal stemware at its hand-carved tasting bar. You can also venture on the deck for a more leisurely glass of wine and cheese pairing.

Travel southwest to Buchanan to reach Tabor Hill Winery and Restaurant, a destination for dining among the vines, within the tasting room or deck side on a gorgeous day. In 2002, David and Linda Upton expanded the original building to encompass a second dining room lined with spacious windows. The restaurant is a premiere destination for high-quality, in-season fare paired with Tabor Hill wines, such as the Classic Demi-Sec, Barrel Select Chardonnay or Red Arrow red wines—longtime customer favorites.

In 2006, Mike and Bob Jacobson of Leelanau Wine Cellars built a modern, airy tasting room of sandy maple interiors, with the exterior painted deep blue like the lake it overlooks. If you arrive by sail, ease into the quaint harbor town and jump out onto the dock for a quick stroll into the tasting room. The spacious tasting room bar provides plenty of elbowroom for sipping wines and enjoying the breathtaking view of stately sailboats gliding by. To soak in the views a little longer, you can sit on the balcony next door at Knot, Just a Bar, where lakeside bar food is generously served.

South of Leelanau Wine Cellars is Willow Vineyards in Suttons Bay with the million-dollar view from its tasting room atop the hill. Lake Michigan blues complement ripe vineyard hues throughout the seasons.

On neighboring Old Mission Peninsula, the gleaming steel tasting room of 2 Lads seems to reflect the sunlight bouncing off Grand Traverse East Bay of Lake Michigan. Just down the road, atop another grand vista, is Chateau Chantal, affording expansive views of both East and West Bays from its tasting room.

For a longer stay, five wineries offer overnight room accommodations in the vineyard, including Chateau Chantal and Chateau Grand Traverse on Old Mission Peninsula, Black Star Farms on Leelanau Peninsula, Pleasantview Vineyards in Harbor Springs and, in southwest Michigan, the Cottage of Lindah, a Victorian-style farmhouse amid the vineyards of Hickory Creek Winery.

FUTURE GROWTH FOR MICHIGAN'S LARGEST WINERIES

Reflecting on growth opportunities in our industry, St. Julian Vintner David Braganini believes the biggest potential for Michigan is within our state.

"All of our growth will likely come from within Michigan," says David.

Michiganders have a sweet palate. Rieslings are tremendous here. Our state can make nice, fruity, cold-climate wines. Our demographic is open-minded. We're attracting a lot of younger people, and we have a strong, young loyal following.

Chris Moersch of Round Barn Winery and Free Run Cellars says they're focusing more on strengthening customer relationships in the tasting rooms as well:

We experienced our company's largest growth in 2009. We've doubled employees, planted more vines and invested in facility improvements. We expect to see our biggest growth come from Michigan because people are sticking closer to home.

On the other hand, two of Michigan's largest wineries, Chateau Grand Traverse and Leelanau Wine Cellars, are seeking growth beyond Michigan.

"Growth for Leelanau Wine Cellars is probably going to come from both within Michigan and beyond. There is a lot of room for growth for all the Michigan wineries," says vintner Bob Jacobson.

Though we are also focusing on neighboring Great Lakes states. It's simply more expensive to sell wine farther away from home than closer. We can ship to an Ohio or Indiana distributor far more easily than a Florida distributor. Similarly, it's easier for us to go work in those markets and help create that growth.

Eddie O'Keefe III, president of Chateau Grand Traverse, also believes growth will come from beyond Michigan:

Our business model is to look at the larger playing field and bring Michigan wines forward on the map to draw people to our market. We've been growing consistently and now have everything in place with our new bottling line to move forward on expanding into ten to fifteen states.

WORLD-CLASS WINES

Michigan wines are gaining notoriety, racking up awards in national and international competitions and building a loyal following of consumers. Michigan wineries are producing an amazing spectrum of both red and white wines from very sweet to very dry.

"Riesling is so conducive to our climate and land, all up and down our western coast," says Joe Borello, co-founder of Tasters Guild International and a Michigan wine judge since the late 1970s. "We have excellent quality Pinot Gris [Pinot Grigio] wines, and Pinot Blancs are doing extremely well. Cabernet Franc is standing out, and I'm really excited about the development of Syrah here."

Domaine Berrien Cellars and Lemon Creek Winery in southwest Michigan are among the few wineries producing Syrah (Shiraz) in the state.

Joe is also excited about the lesser-known Chambourcin wines produced by Fenn Valley, St. Julian and Lemon Creek and believes Michigan is made for sparkling wine production. He acknowledges Larry Mawby's brilliant niche with sparkling wine production and marketing.

Renowned wine critic and writer Tom Stevenson wrote in his book, *The New Sotheby's Encyclopedia of Wine*, that he was "impressed by Michigan Pinot Noirs because of their naturally elegant weight and structure; and by the Pinot Grigios, which typically exceed in quality their Italian namesakes; and by the Merlots, Rieslings, Chardonnays and sparkling wines."

Tom also called Black Star Farms "Michigan's superstar boutique winery" and further credited Black Star Farms' winemaker, Lee Lutes, by stating, "Lutes even manages to bring a touch of class to hybrids, making a yummy Red House Red from a blend of Marechal Foch, Dornfelder, Regent and Cabernet Franc." Perhaps his highest praise was when he referred to Lee as "the state's most-gifted red winemaker."

Winemaker Bryan Ulbrich is gaining a reputation worldwide for his world-class white wines. He's focused on crafting wines from four grape varietals, Riesling, Pinot Blanc, Pinot Grigio and Gewürztraminer. He works with more than a dozen growers who grow grapes for him exclusively on Old Mission Peninsula, Leelanau Peninsula and in Antrim County.

"My growers offer a nice trio of qualities; they own great dirt, they love to work and love to drink wine," says Bryan. "Releasing single-vineyard wines from completely different sites enables us to highlight what these growers are doing." Tom Stevenson highlighted Bryan in his *The Sotheby's Wine Encyclopedia: The Classic Reference to Wines Around the World*, stating that Bryan "produced the first world class Gewürztraminer outside of Alsace in 2002." Alsace is a renowned wine-growing region of France.

Bryan and his wife, Jennifer, own Left Foot Charley and are currently producing thirty-four hundred cases annually with the goal to grow to five thousand to six thousand cases a year. They spent eleven years seeking the perfect location for their tasting room and found it at the historic Northern Michigan Asylum, now the nation's largest preservation project and smartly reappointed the Village of Grand Traverse Commons. Their focus on growing a local following is underscored by their innovative marketing. The winery offers many hands-on cooking events and fun gatherings and also sells one-liter growler bottles to encourage repeat visits to fill up the growler with wine or delicious hard apple cider made from Michigan apples.

"We have Friday growler parades," says Bryan. "Our customers file in to fill up their growlers with whatever 'loose wine' we have available. And it's all top-notch wine made in small batches." Bryan encourages this new way of living. "Come in for a glass of wine or stop by to pick up local wine for a last-minute dinner gathering."

The O'Keefe family of Chateau Grand Traverse is strongly focused on solidifying Michigan's reputation as a producer of world-class European vinifera wines, particularly Rieslings, and they've held this mantra since the mid-1970s. Today, Sean O'Keefe sees a strong trend toward producing wines from grapes grown in a single vineyard rather than from multiple vineyards. Generally, these tend to be smaller bottlings since the fruit derives from a single vineyard. Other winemakers are following this practice as well, including Matt and Chris Moersch at Free Run Cellars, Spencer Stegenga of Bowers Harbor Vineyards and Lee Lutes of Black Star Farms.

Sixteen-year industry veteran Mike De Schaaf of Hickory Creek Winery of Baroda is focused on using the best fruit possible. "If you start with great fruit, you can make great wine." Hickory Creek Winery's first vintage was 2005. The two-thousand-case winery produces dry-style vinifera wines, including Riesling, Chardonnay, Pinot Noir, Cabernet Franc Rosé and Gewürztraminer.

"Wines can be dry without being overly acidic. They can be fruity without being sweet. If you don't want to taste fruit, drink scotch. It's all about producing a wine that is balanced," says Mike. His focus is on encouraging customers to think of wine as food. "Wine should be part of the dinner table."

Mike first started learning about winemaking at Round Barn Winery in 1994, under Rick Moersch, for whom Mike has the highest regard. In 2002, Mike left to start his own business as a vineyard manager. Today, he is teamed with his brother, Jeff De Schaaf, and David Leslie and is producing wines at the trio's Hickory Creek Winery. The vintners are targeting five thousand cases a year for production.

Traverse City–area native Shawn Walters, a seventeen-year wine industry veteran, has produced numerous award-winning wines as a consultant to Chateau Fontaine and start-up wineries, including Longview Winery and 45 North, and as former winemaker for Leelanau Wine Cellars. Shawn also co-produced a wine for Jana Winery with Scott Harvey of Napa Valley and Amador County, California, who says, "Michigan is an up-and-coming region with the ability to produce world-class Rieslings similar to those produced in Germany. Shawn Walters is emerging as the superstar of Michigan winemakers."

Shawn is currently planting his own vineyard on his Leelanau Peninsula farm to produce high-end white wines to further leverage Michigan's reputation as a producer of world-class wines.

Dr. David Miller has been overseeing the vineyards and winemaking for St. Julian for the last thirteen years. "We've raised the bar. We're focused on viticulture; applying techniques such as better trellising, crop control and the plantings of better clones to produce more complex wines. We do a lot of research before we plant, and we follow quality through to the bottling." St. Julian garners numerous awards every year for wines, ranging from Riesling to Blue Heron, with their Solera cream sherry garnering the most awards in the winery's history.

Dr. Charlie Edson of Bel Lago has Michigan's oldest Dijon clone of Pinot Noir, planted twenty-two years ago on his prime vineyard site, 960 feet above sea level, along Lake Leelanau in northwest Michigan. He describes his Pinot Noir as "an elite clone" from the Burgundy region of France. "The best Pinot Noirs rely on this clone." Pinot Noir is a tough, expensive grape to grow in Michigan. It is fickle and has to have prime growing and climate conditions. Many of Michigan's winemakers call Pinot Noir "the heartbreak grape." Charlie uses his Pinot Noir to blend and add to sparkling wine and, in great growing seasons, produce a vintage wine. When Pinot Noir has the right conditions, it's a red wine that stands out.

Charlie speaks to how the industry has evolved over the past twenty-eight years: "We are very focused on viticulture and growing quality grapes. Many of us have been making wine for decades. We have better-quality grapes to work with, and we're experienced."

Year after year, Michigan wines are beating wines from renowned regions in national and international competitions, and in 2008 alone, they achieved more than eight hundred gold, silver and bronze medals. In 2010, 137 Michigan wines were entered in the Tasters Guild International wine competition, a big leap from the 1980s, when a few wineries needed to be persuaded to submit wines for the competition. Today, Michigan winemakers proudly and confidently showcase their wines next to wines from other renowned wine regions from around the world.

MICHIGAN'S WINE LEGACY...AND VIBRANT FUTURE

Michigan's cold-climate wines are uniquely affected by the massive lakes that surround the peninsulas, offering a lively connection to the land. Our wine heritage expresses Michigan's diverse agricultural bounty, its Great Lakes maritime climate and its winemaker skills. Michigan's wine history is woven within the state's agricultural legacy and is an essential ingredient of its vibrant future.

As Eddie O'Keefe III, of Chateau Grand Traverse, concludes, "Wineries give credibility to a region. They give a region soul."

MICHIGAN WINERIES

Southwest Lower Peninsula

Fennville AVA

Fenn Valley Vineyards, Fennville, www.fennvalley.com

Lake Michigan Shore AVA

Cody Kresta Vineyard and Winery, Mattawan, www.codykrestawinery.com
Contessa Wine Cellars, Coloma, www.contessawinecellars.com
Domaine Berrien Cellars, Berrien Springs, www.domaineberrien.com
Founders Wine Cellars, Baroda, www.founderswinecellar.com
Free Run Cellars, Berrien Springs, www.freeruncellars.com
Hickory Creek Winery, Baroda, www.hickorycreekwinery.com
Karma Vista Vineyards, Coloma, www.karmavista.com
Lawton Ridge Winery, Kalamazoo, www.lawtonridgewinery.com
Lemon Creek Winery, Berrien Springs, www.lemoncreekwinery.com
McIntosh Apple Orchards and Winery, South Haven, www.mcintoshorchards.com
Old Shore Vineyards, Buchanan, www.oldshorevineyards.com
Peterson and Sons Winery, Kalamazoo, www.naturalwine.net
Round Barn Winery, Brewery and Distillery, Baroda, www.roundbarnwinery.com
St. Julian Winery Company, Paw Paw, www.stjulian.com

Tabor Hill Winery, Buchanan, www.taborhill.com
Warner Vineyards, Paw Paw, www.warnerwines.com
Wyncroft, Buchanan, www.wyncroftwine.com

Other Areas

Cascade Winery, Grand Rapids, www.cascadecellars.com
Clay Avenue Cellars, Muskegon, www.clayavenuecellars.com
Lake Effect Winery, Grand Haven, www.lakeeffectwinery.com
Robinette Cellars, Grand Rapids, www.robinettes.com

NORTHWEST LOWER PENINSULA

Leelanau Peninsula AVA

Bel Lago Vineyard and Winery, Cedar, www.bellago.com
Black Star Farms, Suttons Bay, www.blackstarfarms.com
Boskydel Vineyard, Lake Leelanau, www.boskydel.com
Chateau de Leelanau Vineyard and Winery, Suttons Bay, www.chateaudeleelanau.com
Chateau Fontaine, Lake Leelanau, www.chateaufontaine.com
Cherry Republic Winery, Glen Arbor, www.cherryrepublic.com
Ciccone Vineyard and Winery, Suttons Bay, www.cicconevineyards.com
Circa Estate Winery, Lake Leelanau, www.circawinery.com
Forty-Five North Vineyard and Winery, Lake Leelanau, www.fortyfivenorth.com
Gill's Pier Vineyard and Winery, Northport, www.gillspier.com
Good Harbor Vineyards, Lake Leelanau, www.goodharbor.com
Leelanau Cellars, Omena, www.leelanaucellars.com
L. Mawby Vineyards, Suttons Bay, www.lmawby.com
Longview Winery, Cedar, www.longviewwinery.com
Raftshol Vineyards, Suttons Bay, www.raftsholvineyards.com
Shady Lane Cellars, Suttons Bay, www.shadylanecellars.com
Silver Leaf Vineyard and Winery, Suttons Bay, www.silverleafvineyard.com
Willow Vineyards, Suttons Bay, www.willowvineyardwine.com

Michigan Wineries

Old Mission Peninsula AVA

Black Star Farms-Old Mission, Traverse City, www.blackstarfarms.com
Bowers Harbor Vineyards, Traverse City, www.bowersharbor.com
Brys Estate Vineyard and Winery, Traverse City, www.brysestate.com
Chateau Chantal Winery, Traverse City, www.chateauchantal.com
Chateau Grand Traverse, Traverse City, www.cgtwines.com
Peninsula Cellars, Traverse City, www.peninsulacellars.com
2 Lads Winery, Traverse City, www.2lwinery.com

Other Areas

Douglas Valley Organic Vineyards, Manistee, www.douglasvalley.net
Fox Barn Market and Winery, Shelby, www.thefoxbarn.com
Jomagrha Vineyards and Winery, Pentwater, www.jomagrha.com
Krolczyk Cellars, Freesoil, www.kcellars.com
Left Foot Charley, Traverse City, www.leftfootcharley.com
Pleasantview Vineyards, Harbor Springs, www.pleasantviewwinery.us
Tartan Hill Winery, New Era, www.tartanhillwinery.com

SOUTHEAST LOWER PENINSULA

Blue Water Winery and Vineyard, Carsonville, www.bluewaterwinery.com
Burgdorf's Winery, Haslett, www.burgdorfwinery.com
Chateau Aeronautique Winery, Jackson, www.chateauaeronautiquewinery.com
Cherry Creek Cellars, Albion, www.cherrycreekwine.com
Cherry Creek Old Schoolhouse Winery, Brooklyn,
    www.oldschoolhousewinery.com
Lone Oak Vineyard Estate, Grass Lake, www.loneoakvineyards.com
Pentamere Winery, Tecumseh, www.pentamerewinery.com
Sandhill Crane Vineyards, Jackson, www.sandhillcranevineyards.com
Sleeping Bear Winery, Albion, www.sleepingbearwinery.com
Trees Cellars, Blissfield, www.treeswines.com
Uncle Johns Fruit House Winery, St. John's, www.fruithousewinery.com
Wolcott Winery, Mt. Morris, www.wolcottwinery.com

NORTHEAST LOWER PENINSULA

Dizzy Daisy Winery and Vineyard, Bad Axe, www.dizzydaisywinery.com
Nicholas's Black River Vineyard and Winery, Cheboygan, www.nicholasblackriverwinery.com
Rose Valley Winery, Rose City, www.rosevalleywinery.net
Stoney Acres Winery, Alpena, www.stoneyacreswinery.net

UPPER PENINSULA

Garden Bay Winery, Garden, www.gardenbaywinery.com
Mackinaw Trail Winery, Manistique, www.mackinawtrailwinery.com
Threefold Vine Winery, Garden, www.mackinawtrailwinery.com

BIBLIOGRAPHY

Adams, Leon D. *The Wines of America*. Boston: Houghton Mifflin Company, 1973.

Adrian County. *Adrian County Directory 1874–5*. Detroit, MI: Burch, Montgomery and Co., 1874.

Arend, Al. "Foreign Grape Research Expanding." *News-Palladium* [Benton Harbor], February 12, 1971.

Bak, Richard. *Cobb Would Have Caught It: The Golden Age of Baseball in Detroit*. Detroit, MI: Wayne State University Press, 1991.

Baxevanis, John J. *The Wine Regions of America: Geographical Reflections and Appraisals*. Stroudsburg, PA: Vinifera Wine Growers Journal, 1992.

Bulkley, John McClelland. *History of Monroe County, Michigan*. Vol. II. Chicago: The Lewis Publishing Company, 1913.

Burton, Clarence Monroe, William Stocking and Gordon K. Miller. "Beginning of Detroit." Chap. 6 in *The City of Detroit, Michigan, 1701–1922*. Vol. 1. Detroit, MI: The S.J. Clarke Publishing Company, 1922.

Catherman, Charles. "St. Julian Wine Company: Michigan's Oldest, Largest Winery Keeps Growing." *Vintner & Vineyard* [Lansing], May 1991.

Childs, Mrs. Edmund. "Recollections of Life in Monroe County, Michigan." Interviews, 1956–1962. Monroe County Library Systems.

Church, Ruth Ellen. "Let's Learn About Wine." *Valley News* [Van Nuys], October 16, 1975.

———. Untitled articles. *Chicago Tribune*, June 23, 1969; June 13, 1974.

Coates, Rick. "Dinner with Mario." *Northern Express* [Traverse City], April 22–May 6, 2010.

Courier-Leader [Paw Paw]. "Grape and Wine Industry Has…" July 2, 1976.

———. Untitled. July 2, 1976.

Daily News [Ludington], September 14, 1998.

Daniels, W.H. *Temperance Reform and Its Great Reformers*. New York: Nelson & Phillips, 1878.

Dennis, F.G., Jr., G.M. Kessler and H. Davidson. *From Seed to Fruit: 150 Years of Horticulture at Michigan State, 1855–2005*. East Lansing, MI: University Printing, 2007.

Detroit Free Press. "Cask Force of One Finds No Sour Grapes." August 24, 1980.

Detroit News. "State Vintner Proudly Donates Product to Mass." August 26, 1987.

Dye, John. "Blaze Linked to Burglary: Fire Damages Wine Firm." *Herald-Palladium* [Benton Harbor], July 25, 1974.

Ellis, J. Dee. *Pioneering Families and History of Lapeer County, Michigan*. Lapeer, MI: Lapeer Genealogy Society, 1981.

Ethridge, David. Untitled article. *Lapeer Area View*, April 4, 2009.

———. "The Wines of Old Lapeer." *Lapeer Area View*, July 2004.

Evening Sentinel [Holland]. "Daily Tours Available at Fennville Winery." July 9, 1976.

Farmington Enterprise. "America's Finest Winery Is Ready Near Farmington." August 16, 1934.

———. "Large Oak Casks Are Put in Place at New Winery." January 4, 1933.

The Farmington Junction Historical Museum. "The La Salle Wine Vats." February 8, 2010. http://www.caravantradingcompany.com/vat.html.

Finkelman, Paul, and Martin J. Herschock. *The History of Michigan Law*. Athens: Ohio University Press, 2006.

Garceau, Kristen. "Reorganization of Warner Vineyards Continues." *Kalamazoo Gazette*, March 28, 1990.

Gentry, Karen. "St. Julian Fires Up Still to Produce Tasty Fruit Brandies." *Fruit Growers News*, July 1999.

Gillard, Kathleen. *Our Michigan Heritage*. New York: Pageant Press, 1955.

Herald-Palladium [Benton Harbor]. "Area Winemakers Mark Sales Hike." N.d.

Herald-Press [St. Joseph]. "Busy Time at Molly Pitcher's: Long, Slow Wine Process Starts with a Rush." October 5, 1960.

———. "96% of Mich Wine Sold Inside State." September 22, 1961.

Howell, Dr. G. Stanley. "Developing a Research Program Near the Climatic Limits of Commercial Vine Culture." Presentation for the American Society for Enology and Viticulture, 2007.

————. "Marechal Foch: It's a Red Variety for All Regions." *Vintner & Vineyard* [Lansing], February 1988.

"How the Grape Gave State a New Industry." Unknown publication [Hartford], 1963.

Iron River Junior Historical Society. *The Rum Rebellion*. Iron River, MI: Jubilee Commemorative Edition, February 20–28, 1970.

Ironwood Daily Globe. "Grape Growing in Michigan a Big Industry." September 27, 1963.

————. "Marquette Federal Commissioner will not issue warrants." February 24, 1920.

————. "Washington Checks Armed Expedition Against Iron River." February 26, 1920.

Jahnke, Pam. "Grand Marshal and Vintner." *Kalamazoo Gazette*, n.d.

"James Warner Named Michigan's 'Small Businessman of the Year.'" Unknown publication, May 19, 1975.

Jennings, John. "Bob's Book Is Full of Fun and History." *Tucson Citizen*, March 4, 1994.

Jones, Linda. "The Growth of Michigan's Wine Industry in the Past Quarter Century." A report to the Michigan Department of Agriculture, October 2006.

Kalamazoo Gazette. "Cask Force of One Finds Wine With Spirit." August 24, 1980.

————. "Frontenac…Table Wine Enhances Meal." October 25, 1982.

————. "Some Salvage as Wine Creates Lake at Lawton." June 7, 1940.

————. "Winemaking…A Way of Life." September 23, 1975.

Lansing State Journal, September 14, 1980.

Lawton Leader. "Hundreds of People Are Now Employed in Grape Harvest." 1939.

Lawton Lions Heritage Community Center. Brochure, 1989.

Lenehan, Mike. "The Grape Escape." *Chicago Reader*, November 23, 1979.

Mansfield, J.B. *History of the Great Lakes*. Vol. 1. Chicago: J.H. Beers & Co., 1899.

Mason, Phillip P. *Rumrunning and the Roaring Twenties*. Detroit, MI: Wayne State University Press, 1995.

May, Allan. "The Michigan Whiskey Rebellion." *Crime Magazine*, June 11, 2008. Available online at www.crimemagazine.com/michiganwhiskeyrebellion.htm.

McMurtrie William. *Report upon the Statistics of Grape Culture and Wine Production in the United States for 1880*. Washington, D.C., 1881.

McQuown, Steve. "Prominent Pair: Community Plans Dinner for Educator, Wine Producer." *News-Palladium* [Benton Harbor], June 22, 1972.

Michigan Commission for the Semi-Centennial Celebration. "The Semi-Centennial of the Admission of the State of Michigan into the Union." Detroit, MI: Detroit Free Press Printing Company, 1886.

Michigan Historical Commission. *Michigan History Magazine* 2 (1918).

Michigan, State of. *Early History of Michigan with Biographies of State Officers, Members of Congress, State Legislatures*. Lansing, MI: Thorpe & Godfrey, State Printers and Binders, 1888.

———. *Michigan: A Guide to the Wolverine State*. New York: Oxford University Press, 1941.

Michigan State Pomological Society. *Annual Report of the Michigan Horticultural Society*. Lansing, MI, 1922.

———. *Annual Report of the Secretary of the State Pomological Society of Michigan*. Lansing, MI: W.S. George & Co., State Printers and Binders, 1872, 1874.

———. *Seventeenth Annual Report of the Secretary of the State Pomological Society of Michigan*. Lansing, MI: Thorpe & Godfrey, State Printers and Binders, 1887.

———. *Seventh Annual Report of the Secretary of the State Pomological Society of Michigan*. Lansing, MI: W.S. George & Co., State Printers and Binders, 1878.

———. *Sixth Annual Report of the Secretary of the State Pomological Society of Michigan*. Lansing, MI: W.S. George & Co., State Printers and Binders, 1877.

———. *Third Annual Report of the Secretary of the State Pomological Society of Michigan*. Lansing, MI: W.S. George & Co., State Printers and Binders, n.d.

"Michigan Wine Grapes." In *Michigan Wine Country*. Wine and Touring Guide. Royal Oak, MI: Hour Custom Publishing, 2010.

Monroe Commercial, September 18, 1873; October 2, 1873.

Monroe County Library. "Bygones of Monroe." July 20, 2009. http://monroe.lib.mi.us/eresearch/recommended_sites/history/bygones_monroe/point_winery.htm.

Monroe Democrat, May 21, 1891.

News-Palladium [Benton Harbor]. "Bronte Wine Company Holds Annual Picnic." July 20, 1949.

———. "Bronte Winery Host to Record Throng in '72." February 26, 1973.

———. "County Wine Firm Marks 20th Year." October 3, 1953.

———. "Experts Sit 'n' Sip Wine in Paw Paw." July 30, 1958.

———. "French Hybrid Grape Interest High." January 12, 1973.

———. "Here Is a Rhubarb to Please Everyone." October 10, 1959.

———. "Keeler Builds New Industry; Grape Winery: Bronte Wine Company Constructs Plant in Village." November 23, 1943.

———. "Keeler Firm Develops 2 New Types of Wine." July 25, 1976.

———. "Keeler Wine Output Booming: Bronte Firm Builds New Addition." June 10, 1955.

———. "Lakeside Winery Plans Weinfest." October 14, 1975.

———. "Misuraca Bankrupt: Paw Paw Wine Firm Is Closed." December 22, 1960.

———. "State's Wine Production Shows Again." February 26, 1940.

———. "Test Michigan Types: Wine Tasters Sit 'n' Sip Wine in Paw Paw." July 30, 1958.

———. "Thousand for Weinfest." September 29, 1976.

———. Untitled. September 11, 1965.

———. "Virginia Wine Will Be Made at Paw Paw." March 6, 1941.

———. "Wine Company Holds Christmas Party at Whitcomb." December 21, 1953.

———. "Wineries to Be Good Market for 45 Grapes." August 9, 1945.

———. "Wineries Use Big Share of Local Grapes." September 29, 1940.

———. "Winery Chateau." June 12, 1974.

———. "Winery Near Fennville Offering Guided Tours." August 10, 1976.

News-Palladium [Lawton]. "Fire Detroys Big Houppert Winery at Lawton; Loss May Total $250,000." June 7, 1930.

———. "Van Buren Area Having Record Grape Season: Importance of Wine Industry Felt in Paw Paw Paw." October 1, 1942.

News-Palladium [Paw Paw]. "Paw Paw Winery Buys Plant of Houppert Firm." May 6, 1943.

New York Times. "Maj. Dalrymple Quits Prohibition Post." October 29, 1920.

Nolan, Jenny. "How Prohibition Made Detroit a Bootlegger's Dream Town." *Detroit Free News,* June 15, 1999.

Nolan, Suzanne. "Monroe Wines Had 'A Very Fine Reputation.'" June 13, 1999.

Norton, Mike. "Local Wines Surprise Experts." *Traverse City Record Eagle*, n.d.

Ohio State Pomological Society. *Annual Report of the Ohio State Horticultural Society*. Vol. 28. N.p., 1873.

Pawlak, Debra Anne. *Farmington and Farmington Hills*. Charleston, SC: Arcadia Publishing, 2003.

Pinney, Thomas. *A History of Wine in America from Prohibition to the Present*. Berkeley: University of California Press, 2005.

———. *A History of Wine in America from Prohibition to the Present*. 2nd edition. Berkeley: University of California Press, 2007.

Reagan, Herb. "Pointe Aux Peaux, Monroe, Michigan." July 17, 2009. www.bigballoonmusic.com/goddardreagan/PointeAuxPeauxhistory.htmd.

Rink, Bernard. "Boskydel Vineyards: Pioneering Wine Grape Production in Northern Michigan." *Vintner & Vineyard* 3, no. 3 (August 1989).

Roush, Matt. "Warner Cutting Juice Packing." *Kalamazoo Gazette*, March 20, 1990.

San Antonio Evening News. "Prohibition Officers May Employ Troops When They Begin Campaign Tonight." February 23, 1920.

San Antonio News. "Dry Force Invades Michigan." February 23, 1920.

Schaetzl, Randall, Joe Darden and Danita Brandt. *Michigan Geography and Geology*. New York: Pearson Custom Publishing, 2009.

Smith, Nick. "Sober MSU Experiment: Wine Rated 'Quite Good." *News-Palladium* [Benton Harbor], January 4, 1974.

Sousa, Lisa. "About Cold Duck." Ezine Articles. March 13, 2010. http://ezinearticles.com/?About-Cold-Duck&id=831473.

Stein, Joel. " Fifty States of Wine." *Time*, August 28, 2008.

Sterling, Albert Mack. *The Sterling Genealogy*. New York: The Grafton Press, 1990.

Time. "Industry: The California Rush." May 1, 1971.

Traverse City Record Eagle. "150 Years: Traverse City Then and Now." N.d.

United States Department of Agriculture. Special Report #35, Report on Insects Injurious to Sugar Cane. Washington, D.C.: Government Printing Officer, 1881.

Vintner & Vineyard [Lansing], August 1987.

Walkerville Times. "Mobsters, Mayhem and Murder." N.d.

Warner, James J., and Pat Warner. "Warner Vineyards Boasts a Long and Celebrated History, and a Champagne Success Story." *Vintner & Vineyard* [Lansing], October 1991.

Weintraub, Boris. "Hybrid Grapes and Microclimate Foster Viticulture in Michigan." *National Geographic*, October 5, 1983.

Wing, Talcott E. *History of Monroe County, Michigan*. New York: Munsell & Company, Publishers, 1890.

Winnepeg Free Press, December 6, 1932.

ABOUT THE AUTHORS

L orri Hathaway and Sharon Kegerreis are authors of the award-winning *From the Vine: Exploring Michigan Wineries* (2007). The native Michiganders share a passion for living and playing along the Great Lakes and exploring wine and food destinations. Researching Michigan's earliest wine pioneers ignited a passion for Michigan's rich agricultural history and has turned

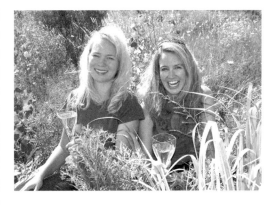

Lorri Hathaway and Sharon Kegerreis. *Photograph by Kristopher Kegerreis.*

the authors into avid historians. They continue to be most intrigued with today's hardworking winemakers and other agriculturalists who inspire them to share their stories. Learn more about the authors and stay tuned for upcoming books at www.michiganvine.com.

Visit us at
www.historypress.net